D1500169

The Kentucky Bicentennial Bookshelf
Sponsored by

KENTUCKY HISTORICAL EVENTS CELEBRATION COMMISSION
KENTUCKY FEDERATION OF WOMEN'S CLUBS

and Contributing Sponsors

AMERICAN FEDERAL SAVINGS & LOAN ASSOCIATION
ARMCO STEEL CORPORATION, ASHLAND WORKS
A. ARNOLD & SON TRANSFER & STORAGE CO., INC. / ASHLAND OIL, INC.
BAILEY MINING COMPANY, BYPRO, KENTUCKY / BEGLEY DRUG COMPANY
J. WINSTON COLEMAN, JR. / CONVENIENT INDUSTRIES OF AMERICA, INC.
IN MEMORY OF MR. AND MRS. J. SHERMAN COOPER BY THEIR CHILDREN
CORNING GLASS WORKS FOUNDATION / MRS. CLORA CORRELL
THE COURIER-JOURNAL AND THE LOUISVILLE TIMES
COVINGTON TRUST & BANKING COMPANY
MR. AND MRS. GEORGE P. CROUNSE / GEORGE E. EVANS, JR.
FARMERS BANK & CAPITAL TRUST COMPANY / FISHER-PRICE TOYS, MURRAY
MARY PAULINE FOX, M.D., IN HONOR OF CHLOE GIFFORD
MARY A. HALL, M.D., IN HONOR OF PAT LEE,
JANICE HALL & MARY ANN FAULKNER
OSCAR HORNSBY INC. / OFFICE PRODUCTS DIVISION IBM CORPORATION
JERRY'S RESTAURANTS / ROBERT B. JEWELL
LEE S. JONES / KENTUCKIANA GIRL SCOUT COUNCIL
KENTUCKY BANKERS ASSOCIATION / KENTUCKY COAL ASSOCIATION, INC.
THE KENTUCKY JOCKEY CLUB, INC. / THE LEXINGTON WOMAN'S CLUB
LINCOLN INCOME LIFE INSURANCE COMPANY
LORILLARD A DIVISION OF LOEW'S THEATRES, INC.
METROPOLITAN WOMAN'S CLUB OF LEXINGTON / BETTY HAGGIN MOLLOY
MUTUAL FEDERAL SAVINGS & LOAN ASSOCIATION
NATIONAL INDUSTRIES, INC. / RAND MCNALLY & COMPANY
PHILIP MORRIS, INCORPORATED / MRS. VICTOR SAMS
SHELL OIL COMPANY, LOUISVILLE
SOUTH CENTRAL BELL TELEPHONE COMPANY
SOUTHERN BELLE DAIRY CO. INC.
STANDARD OIL COMPANY (KENTUCKY)
STANDARD PRINTING CO., H. M. KESSLER, PRESIDENT
STATE BANK & TRUST COMPANY, RICHMOND
THOMAS INDUSTRIES INC. / TIP TOP COAL CO., INC.
MARY L. WISS, M.D. / YOUNGER WOMAN'S CLUB OF ST. MATTHEWS

John Sherman Cooper

The Global Kentuckian

ROBERT SCHULMAN

THE UNIVERSITY PRESS OF KENTUCKY

Research for The Kentucky Bicentennial Bookshelf
is assisted by a grant from the
National Endowment for the Humanities.
Views expressed in the Bookshelf do not
necessarily represent those of the Endowment.

ISBN: 0-8131-0220-0

Library of Congress Catalog Card Number: 76-9514

A statewide cooperative scholarly publishing agency
serving Berea College, Centre College of Kentucky,
Eastern Kentucky University, Georgetown College,
Kentucky Historical Society, Kentucky State University,
Morehead State University, Murray State University,
Northern Kentucky University, Transylvania University,
University of Kentucky, University of Louisville, and
Western Kentucky University.

Editorial and Sales Offices: Lexington, Kentucky 40506

JOHN SHERMAN COOPER

The Global Kentuckian

1

It WAS ONE of those times of high, historic drama in the chamber of the Senate of the United States. The war in Vietnam had dragged on for eight years. They were years which had seen an ever-increasing commitment of United States forces to the conflict until more than a half-million Americans were fighting on the Asian mainland. They were years which had seen the employment of the vast resources of the world's most powerful technological society against half of a small Asian nation; years which had seen, in the face of overwhelming force, little or no abatement of the enemy's will or ability to continue the struggle.

At home more and more Americans were becoming disenchanted with what appeared to them an exercise in futility. Talk of Russian or Chinese support for the other side did not mask the bitter realization that the United States could not use its unlimited might without wiping out an entire people and inflicting horrors inconceivable for a moral society. Shaken to its foundations was America's faith that it could shape the world as it wished to have it. Among many young people the disenchantment had sharpened into outbreaks of violence as it appeared that the government remained unresponsive to their hunger for some tangible sign of ways to disengage the United States from involvement in the war.

Now it was July 24, 1972. Five days earlier, Republican Senator John Sherman Cooper of Kentucky had introduced legislation calling for withdrawal of all American troops from Indochina within four months.

The proposal strikingly lacked the preconditions of a return of American prisoners of war and a cease-fire; these had been set that May in a peace offer to North Vietnam by President Richard M. Nixon, soon to get the GOP's acclaiming nod for a second term. Indeed, the same preconditions had appeared in a proposed amendment to the foreign assistance act by Democratic majority leader Mike Mansfield, for which Cooper's amendment was a substitute. The Kentuckian asked that no authorized or appropriated money be used for anything but the withdrawal of all U. S. forces from Vietnam, Laos, and Cambodia, along with the protection of such forces as they were pulled out. Ward Sinclair, Washington bureau chief for the Louisville newspapers in Senator Cooper's home state, noted that Cooper had introduced his amendment to a nearly empty chamber with little advance notice and without the cosponsorship of any other antiwar senator.

Debate was long and bitter, parliamentary maneuvers tricky. When the Cooper proposal seemed doomed, Senator Edward Brooke of Massachusetts moved to save it by adding a proviso calling for the return of American prisoners of war before a troop pullout. Still, feelings ran high. Senator John O. Pastore of Rhode Island called the Cooper proposal "a shadow of shame on the conscience of America." He went on to say, "If I had a son in a prison in North Vietnam I would think the United States had betrayed him."

Cooper, then seventy-one, stood erect, straightening his horn-rimmed glasses. He responded haltingly, "I say to my dear friend from Rhode Island, you ask what we gain. We gain the end of fighting, the saving of American lives, the foreclosure of more prisoners taken, the end of slaughter of human life. . . . I want someone to tell me how we are going to get our prisoners back if we keep bombing, shelling and strafing Vietnam."

In the end, though the main bill was defeated, Cooper's

troop recall amendment as revised by Brooke won Senate approval. That was counted an epochal event. "At long last we have reached the moment of truth," said New York's Senator Jacob Javits. Exulted Brooke: ". . . an historic occasion, the first true end-the-war amendment passed since the war began." On Cooper's creviced face, an observer thought he saw the look of a man relieved of an enormous burden. Cooper confirmed the impression. "I feel purged inside," he said. "I've felt strongly about this for a long time. Now it's in the hands of the President. He's the only person who can do anything about ending the war now."

Later, enumerating Cooper's major achievements, colleagues and press alike said that no man had done more than Cooper during the entire divisive span of the Vietnam war to reestablish the delicate balance between the Senate and the White House in the making of war and peace. Indeed, Cooper had led in preventing "another Vietnam" by curbing the presidential use of ground troops in Cambodia and Laos, through the Cooper-Church amendments, cosponsored with Idaho's Democratic Frank Church. Recalled also was his leadership in the fight against the production and deployment of antiballistic strategic missiles that he showed were both unneeded and unproved. The limiting of their production and emplacement, later made formal in the first Strategic Arms Limitation Treaty (SALT) agreement between the United States and the Soviet Union, may have saved the world from another nuclear arms race.

Cited, too, was Cooper's effectiveness as ambassador to India and Nepal in 1954 and 1955, where Prime Minister Jawaharlal Nehru made it known that never before had the United States sent so respected and persuasive an emissary. Earlier he had served Democratic President Harry Truman in the establishment of the North Atlantic Treaty Organization. Here his work as a diplomat has been favorably compared to that of Dwight Eisenhower as a military planner in the effort to spur Europe to collaborative economic recovery and military strength against Soviet incursions. Cooper had also served at the United Nations and on secret fact-finding missions to India and Russia for a newly elected John F. Kennedy. In these missions he had won the grudging respect, even the trusting admiration, of the likes of Russia's President Anastas I. Mikoyan and India's Krishna Menon.

Then in 1974, Cooper was nominated by President Gerald Ford and swiftly approved by the Senate as first United States ambassador to the communist German Democratic Republic. Cooper's arrival to establish an embassy marked the first formal U.S.-East German relationship across the Berlin wall since the superpowers of Washington and Moscow had faced each other at flashpoint tension in the early 1960s. At the swearing-in, September 20, 1974, Secretary of State Henry Kissinger said, "He is the right man for an extraordinarily difficult assignment . . . the amelioration of tension and improvement of relations between east and west."

Yet the man thus known in statecraft and the urbane world of diplomacy came from a state whose people for three-quarters of a century have averaged among the nation's lowest in literacy, in income, and, perhaps most significant in this context, in their acceptance of enlightened internationalism. There could scarcely be a wider gulf than the one between the protocols of Whitehall and the fractious, backslapping politics of Whitesburg, Kentucky. What circumstances, what forces made this man Cooper accomplished alike in the drawing rooms of Paris and the courthouses of Kentucky, the government chambers of New Delhi and the hollows of Appalachia? Was it accident or experience? Or was there also a special heritage, a regional melding of disparate elements that led this Kentuckian to national and international achievement?

There was little in his early life to forecast his cosmopolitan eminence. Somerset, Kentucky, spawned John Sherman Cooper. It is a town of 11,000 in the lee of the state's eastern mountains where Republicanism, like Southern Baptistry, always tended to be unreconstructed. It was and is part of a Republican oasis in a commonwealth otherwise so traditionally Democratic that in his time atheist Robert Ingersoll said he'd believe in a hell if Kentucky ever went Republican. By outsiders Cooper has, with persistent error, been described as "a mountain man." Actually, Somerset is nestled in the foothills between Kentucky's Bluegrass country and its Cumberland Mountains and, home folks are wont to say, shares the characteristics of each—the taciturn insularity of the hills, the flossier traditions of the horse counties. The mountain side of the combination accounts in Cooper's speech for his saying "fella," "gov'ment," "gret" for "great" and "hepin' " for "helping."

In politics, Cooper's campaign mode was traditional old-boy Kentucky; he walked up and down the streets of such towns as Viper, Dwarf, Cadiz, and Stamping Ground shaking hands with all who'd do that with a Republican; he made small talk on courthouse steps with one-gallus hangers-on about tobacco price supports, coal prices, and kinfolk. But not about international relations. As a candidate for the Senate, it took him five attempts before winning a full term he could call his own. In 1946 and again in 1952 and 1956 he won election to the unexpired terms of others but did not enjoy his first six-year term until 1960 when he was fifty-nine (although then, and again in 1966, he garnered the largest majorities ever given a Kentucky statewide candidate).

In the Senate, the floor style of the mild-mannered, soft-spoken Cooper frequently was described as ranging from the mumbled to the inaudible. Once, it is said, reporter Spencer Rich of the *Washington Post* almost fell from the press gallery while leaning forward with cupped ear to distinguish a Cooper remark. Moreover, Cooper never mastered or showed much interest in one game played by most other senators, that is, promoting their accomplishments through press releases and press conferences. Cooper gave little thought to such tactics even when it might have meant added public support for a legislative goal. The result, as *Commonweal* magazine noted in 1954 when Cooper was vainly trying to hold a senate seat against the challenge of former Vice President Alben Barkley, was "a comparatively obscure national image . . . at variance with his record." In 1960, when *Newsweek* magazine polled fifty Washington correspondents to name the ablest persons in Congress, the choice of Cooper as the ablest Republican in the Senate was tagged as "the surprise" of the story.

But on October 17, 1972, there occurred in the Senate a remarkable event: a chronicling of the character and achievements of the man from Somerset. After the second longest cumulative service of any senator from Kentucky in the commonwealth's history despite the two interruptions by defeat, John Sherman Cooper had announced he would not run again. In a chamber where "distinguished" and "honorable" are as commonly used as "partisan" and "political," more than two dozen senators of every ideological shading took the floor on that October day to say farewell to a colleague they regarded as one of the great and most cherished U.S. senators of all time.

It was almost too laudatory to be true and New York's conservative Senator James Buckley took note of this. Said Buckley, "It is customary on such occasions, I know, to praise our departing colleagues in the most glowing terms . . . there is much in such tributes that is heartfelt, but much also that is fluff and tinsel. But today, it is different. The praise will come forth and the good works of John Cooper will be extolled; but the difference will be that absolutely everyone will mean absolutely every word he says. For the truth is that no member of this body has more friends and fewer enemies than has the distinguished senior senator from Kentucky."

Senator Ted Kennedy reevoked the delineation by Lincoln of an earlier Kentuckian, Henry Clay, as "my beau ideal of a statesman"; Kennedy said he could think of no man in the Senate in recent years warranting that title of "beau ideal" as much as John Cooper. Among others who rose on that day to pay tribute were Barry Goldwater of Arizona, James Allen of Alabama, Charles Percy of Illinois, and Philip Hart of Michigan.

His colleagues spoke of some of Cooper's achievements in domestic as well as in foreign policy, reflecting their admiration of his independence and breadth of interest. In 1947—his first senate year—he had joined the late Senator Robert Taft and three others in developing the first legislation for federal aid to education. Despite representing a border state he took an early leadership role in espousing and introducing antidiscrimination bills and principles before the Lyndon Johnson administration put them into statute form in the 1964 Civil Rights Act. He had been among the first to speak out against Wisconsin Senator Joseph McCarthy's disregard of the protections of law for individuals during the Red Scare days of the early 1950s. In spite of Kentucky's being an essentially rural state, Cooper had joined with Maine's Senator Edwin Muskie to push through the Senate the first authorization ever for the use of highway trust fund money for urban mass transit.

Respect came for Cooper's frequent breaks with party discipline and administration desires, even when there was a Republican in the White House. Senator John Stennis of Mississippi said, ". . . as much as any other member of the Senate I have known, and more than any of us, he has really made an extraordinary effort to cast every vote and every speech on the basis of what he believed to be right and just and the best thing for our country as he saw it." Later, the now-retired Senator George Aiken of Vermont, one of Cooper's longtime seatmates, was to say in a letter, "As a Republican Party man John Cooper was, if anything, worse than I was and that was pretty unpredictable."

Another of Cooper's Senate confreres did use the occasion of the farewell to cast an amiable dig at the Kentuckian's notorious habit of procrastination. But naturally, this time of testimonials was no time for anyone to spell out the administrative shambles in which his Senate office specialized—contravened by a devoted staff that always seemed to be suffering from hero worship. Indeed, the worst that could be said of him was the insufferably long time he took for important decisions—and his perennial refusal to act as many thought a border-state Republican should.

Neither, of course, did any of the senator's praising comrades mention historical embarrassments, such as Cooper's failure in 1964 to add his vote to the lonely two cast against the Gulf of Tonkin resolution that paved the way for massive U.S. troop involvement in Vietnam.

But even in this context Cooper frustrated the detractor or the critic bent upon finding serious chinks in the man's armor. It was he who in 1975, looking back upon the matter of the Tonkin Gulf resolution, volunteered his own confession of error: "I do think a more consistent position for me would have been to vote against the resolution for, as the record shows, I was clearly aware at the time that it could lead the nation into war if President Johnson made the choice.

"I think my reasoning was that as President he had already sent thousands of United States forces to Vietnam and I believed they should be protected. Perhaps that was a rationalization."

The other senators sought on that farewell day 1972 to find a touchstone to the composition of character that had produced all this.

"The remarkable thing is that John Sherman Cooper's arguments could have considerable bite to them, and indicated he felt very deeply. Nevertheless, whether we were in agreement or in opposition, discussion thereafter proceeded at a cooler, more even pace. I suppose John Cooper personifies the skill of that famous breed known as 'border politicians'; that is a certain gentlemanly geniality which the Senate has always prized." That was Colorado Senator Gordon Allott's notion.

Clifford Case of New Jersey noted his perseverance and acuity. Cooper "can get to the heart of a matter . . . and he sees it through . . . even to the point of stubbornness sometimes. This is an element of strength for him and for us. It is maddening, of course, sometimes to have to deal with him. He takes a long time, sometimes, to make up his mind but that is because he is careful. We know that when he reaches a decision it is a decision worth waiting for." But Case did not stop without commenting on Cooper's patriotism, from which Case said so many of them had taken inspiration. "His is not the kind of flag-waving business that often passes for patriotism though, in one sense, flag waving is part of it—that is to say, the traditional observance of the rituals of remembrance of times past and things gone by and historical events and people." Case noted his "love of his own place, his state, the creeks and mountains and lovely country as well as the blighted areas. . . . He has never been ashamed to express his reverence for the heroes of his state. This is a wonderful thing especially at a time when so many influences seem to be tearing down the traditions that are an inseparable part of what we are." Case hastened to add, "But this is not a blind adherence to country or to place or even to friends . . . it is a deep feeling that because of what we, at our best, stand for, he is fond of us. So he never hesitates to try to make us better—our country, his state, even in his very sensitive way, ourselves." In the end, among all the senators, Case probably came closest to the essence with his references to Cooper's intellectual and emotional attachment to the heritage and humor of a Kentucky tradition.

It has been defined. It exists. It has played a significant part in the combination that lifted John Sherman Cooper to distinction. It is what allowed him time and again to stand against opposition without losing his opponents' respect: as he did not lose it among adversaries at the United Nations or among the leaders of India or the Soviet Union. Among the senators who fought established policy on Vietnam, he was one of the few not crossed off the "acceptable list" at the White House or the Central Intelligence Agency.

To begin with, Cooper has been steeped in what Kentucky historian A. D. Kirwan said is the "variety of cultural and historic traditions, color and richness that [makes Kentucky] a microcosm of the nation as a whole." Cooper himself tried to pinpoint some of these qualities in what he calls a "somewhat rhetorical" 1948 speech to the Kentucky Society of New York, composed of native Kentuckians gone Gotham.

"We would not be true Kentuckians if . . . we did not believe that [our state's] history, traditions and folklore make it a land set apart from others," he said.

What are the elements, the characteristics of the Kentuckian, Cooper asked.

"At home, he may not have reached that level of material accomplishment, of social progress, of social security, or planned mediocrity which seems to occupy our interest today.

"He may not be always conscious of his own attributes and characteristics, but in the perspective of history I do not believe that I exaggerate or oversimplify when I say that his background, his interests and his influence are important because they have expressed principles upon which our concepts of free men and representative government are based."

The Kentuckian was the first and, in spirit, the continuing pioneer of America's western land, Cooper said. In 1790, Kentucky's constitutional convention, encouraged by Thomas Jefferson, adopted the celebrated Kentucky resolutions that protested against the Alien and Sedition Acts that gave power to the president to restrain the civil liberties of aliens and even of states. Kentucky's constitution was the first in the world to grant voting rights without restrictions to all free men (and in 1859 women's suffrage was considered for inclusion in its third rewriting). Early lawlessness spawned by frontier living gave way in time, Cooper said, to a commitment to freedom tied to law.

"The Kentuckian may be reserved, diffident, backward, but in his attitude and demeanor there is no subservience," said Cooper. "It never occurs to the resident of the mountains, the Bluegrass, the Pennyrile or the Purchase [all sections of Kentucky] that he is not as good as any other man. This is a characteristic that residents of other states do not always understand."

All these elements of pride, hardihood and fealty to law Cooper took with him into the councils of the nation and the world. He also took the wit born of pioneer stock. As a Republican in a Democratic state, he learned to listen carefully to others and to turn their sallies on himself. He is fond of recalling the occasion when his proffered campaign handshake was rejected by the old descendant of one of Kentucky's pro-South citizens, still indignant at the state's loyalty to the Union in the Civil War. "No sir," the old man said, ignoring the Cooper hand. "First thing is, you're a Republican. Second thing is, you got a middle name like your daddy, which is Sherman."

To be sure, the Kentucky tradition that in the past gave the nation Henry Clay, the original Cassius Marcellus (Bowie Knife) Clay, nine Supreme Court justices, one president and four vice presidents and a Cooper, also has produced charlatans, poseurs, super-salesmen, super-pols, and super-egos.

The romantic lures of the Kentucky mystique have misled some of the best observers into quicksand. The beloved reporter and folk-tale columnist of the *Louisville Courier-Journal*, Joe Creason, in his final published effort for a sister paper, the *Louisville Times*, startlingly lumped Cooper with three other "giants" of modern-day Kentucky: Harland Sanders, the fried-chicken man; A. B.

(Happy) Chandler, former governor, senator, and national baseball commissioner; and Adolph Rupp, the successful and now retired basketball coach at the University of Kentucky. Accomplished this trio has been—and Cooper and Chandler are close and longtime friends—but with a degree of self-promotion that Cooper never exhibited.

Cooper was raised in a home where the stress was on schooling and where, until the 1920s, there was the wealth to support it. Always bookish as well as athletic, he was graduated, after a year at Centre College, from Yale where his class of 1923 voted him "best liked" and "most likely to succeed"; he put in two years at Harvard Law School before financial reverses at home forced him to drop out. Cooper acquired there the polish to prepare him for later years in the temples of diplomacy traditionally dominated by men from the eastern seaboard—men with the names of Dulles, Acheson, Harriman, Dillon, Bruce, and Bundy.

Yet time and again, it was Cooper's down-home "affidavit face" that people noted, his homely humor, his unpretentiousness that backed up the workings of a careful, compassionate, sifting mind. Before moving to the national and international scene he spent eight years during the depression of the 1920s as county judge—chief administrative officer of his home county. Senator Aiken said in 1974, "I have always thought of John Cooper as one of those rare beings who is a judge in the real sense of the term."

One day, shortly before his departure for East Berlin in December 1974 to take up his duties as ambassador to the German Democratic Republic, Cooper mused about the "Kentucky effect"—Salem cigarette butt in hand, twinkling eyes belying his customary basset-hound look. "At the UN, or in India, I rarely found anyone who hadn't at least heard of Kentucky," he said. "By that, I mean with an unexpected sense of romantic attachment. Some knew about horses. Some knew about 'My Old Kentucky

Home.' But they knew, and it established a little, beginning bond."

That good Kentucky bond tied John Sherman Cooper to an abiding sense of humanism in the most powerful arenas, seeking honorable rapprochement amid deadly national rivalries. A world's quest for peace and justice was aided by the involvement of a good, plain man who never lost touch with his taproots. They helped make him truly a global Kentuckian.

2

IT HAS BECOME more difficult for people to find their growing hopes and aspirations expressed in an industrializing world, so in impatience they turn to the totality of the state—at the expense of freedom," John Sherman Cooper told an interviewer in 1974. "They turn unhappily and wrongly to power, force and coercion."

He added, "Diplomacy is the process of trying to avoid that loss of freedom by finding common, mutual ground between your own interests and the other fellow's. It is often a slow process. But we Kentuckians and other Americans who know what our families and our fathers went through—we know that the slow appeal to man's sense of justice, to his personal and spiritual responsibility, to freedom, has a quality that has always triumphed. It will again, if it is used."

Mixed in with the shrewd common sense of that view of diplomacy is Cooper's almost overwhelming faith in the power of person-to-person relationships. He found it first in a sense of family, of clan, that abides in Kentucky as perhaps nowhere else in the nation.

In 1954 he joined some thousand kin and friends at a reunion of the family of his mother, Helen Gertrude Tartar, whose forebears had migrated from Virginia to Kentucky in the 1780s. The reunion attracted Tartars (sometimes spelled Tarters) from six Kentucky counties, including Cooper's home county of Pulaski, and from five states. As a news account said of the reunion in the

Pulaski County Park, "The Tarter-Tartar women served an abundant dinner to all. In addition to the choicest viands, that they know so well how to prepare, there was barbecued three-year-old beef and a big kettle of rich burgoo"—the latter, of course, the conglomerate stew that is a Kentucky specialty.

By then Cooper already had behind him at the national level two partial Senate terms and service at the UN and with NATO. Speaking at the reunion, he said, "I experience the keenest joy in this opportunity to mingle with so many people of my own blood, and their relatives and friends. It is difficult to describe the sensations that are mine when I see before me so many that share with me the same forefathers.

"Other calls and appeals have kept me away from you but not a day passes that I do not think of you. It was from you and all the people of Pulaski County that I learned the great lesson, that the worthwhile thing in this world is the people, and that their welfare and happiness count the most."

He recalled his years in the 1930s as Pulaski County judge. "In a period of poverty, stress and fear, I discovered that the human touch holds the magic of restoration and the miracle of security," Cooper said. "There I learned that old fashioned kindness has healing in its wings. I can never get away from [those] lessons. They have overshadowed with their appeal and admonition every high place in which I have stood."

Prosperity, not poverty, cloaked Cooper's growing-up. The family was one of the county's wealthiest. His father, the senior John Sherman Cooper, had ancestors, Malachi and Edward Cooper, who had crossed the mountains through the Cumberland Gap from South Carolina around 1790; he owned timber and farm lands and coal mines and was organizer and first president of the Farmers Bank of Somerset. The tall, senior Cooper was a University of Kentucky law graduate, but he did not have much taste for law practice. He turned instead, in this pocket of Kentucky Republicanism, to positions of influence in the Kentucky political scheme: county school superintendent, collector of internal revenue under President Theodore Roosevelt, chairman of the solidly Republican congressional district—and, eventually, county judge as had the father of the spunky Helen Gertrude Tartar, a teacher thirteen years his junior whom he married in 1899.

She and John Senior already had a daughter, Fostine, when John Sherman was born on August 13, 1901. After them came Margaret, Don, Helen, Mary, and Richard. In later years Don, an honor graduate of Yale Law School, and Dick, operator of a stone quarry in which Senator Cooper has an interest, acted for their brother in keeping things straight in his campaign finances; the sisters found themselves involved in door-to-door canvassing for votes.

Naming the first son "Sherman" reflected the section's Civil War slant toward the Union (the senior Cooper had a short-lived half brother named Grant). Yet in Somerset's county park there stands a statue of Confederate General Felix Kirk Zollicoffer, an officer so "pathetically nearsighted," according to historian Bruce Catton, that he met his death in the battle of Mill Springs near Somerset by riding into the middle of a Union regiment. Senator Cooper was influenced by the Kentucky penchant for seeing values North and South; many years later he spoke feelingly of the statue erected at Chickamauga by Kentucky to its dead—different from that of all other states because it commemorated the dead of both sides. Though proudly noting Kentucky's role in the resolutions written by Thomas Jefferson against the Alien and Sedition Acts, Cooper once acknowledged wryly that his family's Civil War opposition to secession was an awkward departure from the states' rights delineated in the resolutions.

John Sherman and his brothers and sisters grew up on Harvey's Hill along Somerset's North Main Street, in a big white frame house, only seven doors up from the Dick

Cooper house that the senator now calls home when he is in Somerset. Respect, duty, and attention to schooling were, along with comfort, the hallmarks of life at the big house. Tall, handsome, immaculately dressed Father Cooper was the commanding figure, but his wife, whom he always called "Mrs. Cooper," wielded the switch and imposed the discipline. It was she who corralled the children when it was time for Mr. Cooper to lead them to the family pew at Somerset's First Baptist Church. There, as the youngsters grew into their courting years, he once sternly informed the minister he would *not* have them turned out of the church for dancing.

Among the brood, it was John who most felt his mother's discipline. Always a reader, he was eternally late for chores, only to be found on a back stairway or in the attic with a book. "My first memory of John is under a tree with a book," says brother Dick who remembers their mother saying once, "What *will* happen to that boy?" John read all the Henty stories and the Frank and Dick Merriwell books and by the age of twelve, he himself recalls, already had finished *Vanity Fair*. For recreation in later life, his reading became Edmund Burke, Spinoza, and Santayana. "I know that sounds heavy, but I also liked H. G. Wells' *Outline of History* and plenty of political stuff," says Cooper.

Because of their father's low opinion of public schools—ironic but shrewdly realistic for a county school executive—schooling for all the children except Dick, the youngest, was conducted privately by a neighbor, Mrs. Anna Mourning, who at one time had four Coopers among her seven pupils. It was the fifth grade before John knew public schooling. His mother took advantage of Father Cooper's absence on a business trip to send John off in a Buster Brown collar and knickers, carrying an umbrella; it took several fights for John to demonstrate that he was not a pantywaist.

In fact, backyard gymnastics frequently competed with reading as Cooper's escapes from doing the chores. Although milking the cow in the barn back of the home and tending the family garden were things John says he did master, the family disagrees. "I could and did milk the cow until Don came along, willing and able—or unwilling but able," the senator genially insists. In any case, it is agreed that his procrastination about chores was the result of what proved to be his lifelong preoccupation with what seemed more important matters.

From boyhood on, Cooper's absentmindedness about schedules was so chronic that among his high school graduation citations was one for a perfect record for tardiness. His inattention to mundane personal needs was such that his two brothers and four sisters agree, "It always took fifteen people to take care of John." (In later life, becoming a chain smoker but always needing to cadge, he is known to have borrowed a lighter and then absentmindedly thrown it out a car window.)

His sister Fostine says, "People were always wanting to help John out, he looked so helpless." On the newspaper route the boys had, brother Don did the collections. When it was time to drive the coal wagon to which the boys were assigned one year, John would call, "Don, go hitch up," and Don obligingly would go hitch up the horse. A quarter-century later, when John Sherman Cooper, then forty-one, returned home on his first leave as a World War II private, the family was astonished to see him followed off the train by a grizzled master sergeant happily hauling the Cooper barracks bag and bidding the tall soldier a cheerful goodbye before reboarding. Yet in the years under the senior Cooper, attendance to needs of others was held in the family like a code of honor. "At Thanksgiving and Christmas or whenever else he saw need, Father would send coal or food into people's basements, telling nobody," Fostine recalls.

At Somerset High School, where John played football and basketball with the "Briar Jumpers," his long skinny legs earned him the nickname of "Bird Legs" (along with "Snipe") and the running gag was that he needed three pairs of long socks at one time, to cover the lengthy limbs. As a senior in 1918, he was on the football and basketball teams, captain of his military training unit, president of his class, and class poet. Despite the regular presence in the home of such newspapers as the now-defunct Cincinnati *Times-Star* owned by the Taft family and, from Louisville, the *Courier-Journal* and its rival of those years, the *Herald-Post,* the overseas world was an alien concept. And yet John's commencement oration was on "The German Spy System." He was seventeen.

From high school Cooper went on to a year at Centre College at nearby Danville. Today, as since its beginning in 1819, it is one of Kentucky's most vigorous private colleges of academic quality, but in 1918 it was mostly known as the home of football's "Prayin' Colonels" with whom Cooper played that year and who, in 1921, captured national headlines by toppling unbeaten Harvard. Cooper, today an emeritus trustee (brother Don is on the board, as Dick is at the University of Kentucky), did not stay at Centre. In 1919, again because of his father's desire that he broaden his education, he switched to Yale. There he occasioned campus laughs by turning out for freshman football in his garish white and gold Centre uniform. It was the Kentuckian's first exposure to the milieu of the eastern prep-school boy. He says now, "I didn't understand it. Frankly, I thought it snobbish."

But he made the team. And self-effacing genuineness won. Four years later Cooper was named "best-liked," as well as "most likely to succeed." He was elected to the elite Skull and Bones senior society and became the first Yalie ever to captain the basketball team in both his junior and senior years. However, to his regret, he did not make Phi Beta Kappa.

One of his classmates was Stuart Symington, later to be a senate colleague across the aisle, on the Democratic side. "It's extraordinary, even hard to believe, that one can know a man for over a half century and still have no criticism of him," Symington said in 1971 on the occasion of a medal awarded to Cooper by Louisville's Catholic Bellarmine College. "But that's true of John Sherman Cooper. He is far and away the most distinguished member of that Yale class."

After Yale, it was Harvard Law School. But in the summer of 1924, after his first year, his father died, with a last wish that John take over as head of the family. Cooper discovered that the 1920 recession had left his father deep in debt. The Somerset commitments called Cooper home after one more year, and he was able to win certification for admittance to the bar only by passing a Kentucky state examination in 1928, a procedure then proper but no longer allowed. It was to take him until 1950 to get family finances into the black. While he liquidated his father's business ventures and sold the family home, moving everyone into a more modest house, his mother returned to teaching. Having only a high school education, she began attending college summer school and taking some correspondence school training; by the time she retired from teaching at seventy, she lacked only technical requirements for a university degree.

Still struggling with the family's financial burdens, Cooper finally hung up his lawyer's shingle in 1928 and ran into hometown habits. He tells what happened when a fellow townsman rushed in one day to describe how his car had just been rammed and he had been injured.

"It sounds to me like you've got an open-and-shut case," Cooper said, visions of a first good client dancing in his head.

"I know, Johnny, I know," the man said. "Now, can you tell me where I can get me a good lawyer?"

Politics and public service, deep in the family fabric, were inevitable. After all, in addition to his father and his maternal grandfather, five earlier Coopers and maternal relatives had been county judges in Pulaski County and two had been circuit court judges, while others had served in the state legislature. In 1927, John Sherman Cooper chose the traditional occasion of "court day" to offer himself as the Republican candidate for the lower house of the state's General Assembly. "Court day" was the first day of the spring term of Circuit Court when custom dictated that the presiding judge followed routine business by opening the courtroom to a day of political talk. When Cooper announced, the cheer that went up from the onlookers wasn't for him, Cooper has always said, "it was for my father."

Elected to the two-year term without opposition, Cooper served at the biennial session in a way that showed his independent streak. "Already, nobody could make him vote for what he didn't think right," his brother says. Don Cooper, then a student at Centre College, says the incumbent governor, Flem Sampson, even telephoned him about persuading John to support a political reorganization of the state's medical-health department. Says Don Cooper, "I told him John wouldn't countenance that, and besides I felt the same way about it John did." He adds wryly, "That was not the year I was made a Kentucky colonel." The bill lost by one vote. Senator Cooper later said, "Flem Sampson never failed to support me, and we became good friends."

Clay Wade Bailey, longtime patriarch of state capital newsmen, told John Ed Pearce of the *Louisville Courier-Journal & Times Sunday Magazine* in 1972 that the dance floor was where the young Cooper made his biggest impression during that initial political fling. "He was tall and handsome and an elegant dresser. Very courtly, you know, gallant. He was always popular with the women."

Cooper has never disavowed the social bouquets. Indeed, he says, "I don't think I made any great mark in the Kentucky House." Yet his vote that helped keep the state's health program out of politics was among only three from the Republican side. He was a strong supporter of the measure that for the first time provided free textbooks to Kentucky school children. And it was freshman legislator Cooper who introduced a bill—it drew no support—to prohibit injunctions against strikes, an early forerunner of the Norris-LaGuardia bill that was later passed by Congress and is law today.

The legislature was prelude to Cooper's eight years as county judge. These years stamped compassion into his being and his experiences then made themselves felt long afterward in the Congress and in diplomacy affecting millions of victims of war and famine.

A surreptitious 1929 document opposing Cooper's candidacy that year for county judge gives a flavor of the Kentucky league in which Cooper was playing. At the time, other Cooper kinfolk were holding or seeking other posts: Roscoe C. Tartar, presiding circuit court judge; John M. Weddle, former sheriff, jailer; Chris L. Tartar, postmaster; Galen E. Jasper, master commissioner; and Jerome E. Tartar, regional head of the federal alcohol tax unit.

Cooper's announced social views were at sharp variance with the conservative attitudes of most of these kin, but that did not deter the authors of the campaign document. It was entitled "Cutting Your Wisdom Teeth" and suggested what a Cooper election would portend:

"First you will be taken before the County Court presided over by Nephew John. When he gets through with you, you will be taken up stairs before Uncle Roscoe. After Uncle Roscoe has worked on you he will deliver you over to Uncle John M.; while Uncle John M. has charge of you, Uncle Chris will handle your mail; when your land is sold, Cousin Gale, Master Commissioner, will attend to that; if you violate the Prohibition Laws, Uncle Jerome will look after you.

"After you have been worked by these and other members of the family, you will feel dam [sic] poor, but you will know that you have cut your wisdom teeth."

Cooper was not to be deterred by such sniping. He walked every byway of the hilly county, pumping hands and grasping shoulders, telling funny stories about those kinfolk and himself. The incumbent was president of a Somerset bank and had been the senior Cooper's law partner, and nobody gave the young slow-talking Cooper much of a chance. But on election night, with Somerset's courthouse square packed, the results showed a handy Cooper victory.

He walked into the little office of the county judge occupied by so many Coopers and kinsmen before him, and into the role of Good Samaritan, social worker, relief-giver. The depression broke the county, left thousands with no means of support and the county judge as the only visible source of succor. "It almost killed him," says Dick Cooper. "He could see misery and need. He could see desperation among people he'd grown up with." Cooper himself has said, "The wrongly maligned WPA saved the county, as it did people throughout the nation."

The county judge's salary was a scarcely munificent $2,500 a year; stories are current in Somerset among those who knew the depression that, when able, Cooper emptied his own pockets for families up against it. Families for whom the law dictated eviction by Judge Cooper turned up on the lawn of the Cooper home, where the judge would somehow manage to find them other quarters. "He had us functioning like a hotel and cafe," says Fostine, with salty equanimity. People began to call him "the poor man's judge."

Cooper's sister Margaret had married a local dentist, William Converse, who soon became accustomed to people coming to his office with a note reading something like, "This man's broke. Pull his tooth. (signed) John."

In 1954 Cooper recalled for a *Time* magazine reporter what it was like in his county office on a cold morning. As many as thirty people crowded in the place, which had his desk and a potbellied stove in opposite corners. "Early in the morning everybody would cluster close up around the stove until it got hot. Then, as the stove got red, the heat pushed them back in a big circle that filled up the whole room" until they pressed against Cooper's desk. "When the circle closed up tight again, I'd know it was time to get up and put in more coal."

Saturdays, when rural folk came to town, Cooper wrote little chits affording the empty-pocketed an austere meal for twenty-five cents at a local eatery, chits which Cooper personally picked up later. The restaurant owner called the quarter meal "the big dinner pail." Mornings, a crowd waited to accompany the lanky young judge on his unhurried way to work and sometimes it took him an hour to walk the few blocks to the courthouse.

Although Lorraine Cooper knows that period only through the memories of her husband and of those she's met who grew to revere him, she assesses the eight depression years as the wheel on which Cooper's basic political philosophy was formed. "From those encounters every day with misery and wounded pride and the actions of people under stress came the understanding of the wants, needs and hopes of others that shaped his entire future life," Mrs. Cooper says. "I think his sensitivity to it was also sharpened by the fact that he was straining to meet his own family's reverses after youthful years of their having had it all going their way."

Another factor for his later success also came from those years, she thinks. "More than ever, he learned to listen," she says. "In recent years he's told me 'always listen, you learn so much.' If it's a person with a problem or an unfriendly country you're dealing with, or one with a position antagonistic to your own, John has said, listen— because in some things you may not have thought of, *they* may be right. Even though you don't change your own position or principle a crumb, even in politics, at least you can assess and report in an unbiased way."

Cooper's own assessment of the county judge years was told a reporter in 1954: "In that job, you get to know everybody and everybody comes to you loaded down with their troubles: the petty offenders, the sick who can't get into hospitals, the unemployed. They all needed advice and help of one sort or another. You learn that everyone—the rich and poor, the high and the unfortunate—everyone has problems." Cooper added on that occasion, when he'd already served a pair of two-year senate stints, "I've been criticized for my votes on 'social bills' but I saw those people in the worst years of the depression and I've never forgotten it. As Justice Holmes said, 'We are all just above despair.' "

Neither did Cooper ever forget the accumulation of down-home anecdotes that were to serve him so well in defusing tense moments at the United Nations. One of these was when he recalled what occurred at the usual preelection day rally in the Somerset town square when he was running for his second term as county judge in 1933.

"Some of the most ardent supporters and antagonists got into a fight and quite a number of them were placed in the pokey. Later that day one of my friends and supporters came to my office and said, 'Judge, I have a list here of our friends I want you to release from jail.'

"I looked at it and I said, 'I think there are more in jail than that and I plan to release all of them this afternoon when tempers have quieted down.'

" 'Oh no,' he said, 'I just want you to release our friends. Let the rest stay!' " Of course the judge freed them all.

In 1939, at the age of thirty-eight, Cooper felt he was ready for bigger challenges and tried for the Republican nomination for governor. "I went all over the state and walked the streets and went in every place," he remembered. "At a time, with Franklin Roosevelt in the White House, when it was the Republican party tactic to denounce everything and, you know, Roosevelt personally, I didn't do that." What he did was talk state issues. While his opponent was saying he would manage finances so well that there would be money aplenty for $30 a month pensions for everyone, Cooper stressed taking state institutions out of politics and running the commonwealth within its existing budget.

The *Louisville Courier-Journal*, Kentucky's statewide paper, said in a Sunday rotogravure spread that Cooper was part of "a merry-hearted and extensive clan of brothers and sisters and a gentle mother," and "when he walks along the street in this city [of Somerset] it is like Old Home Week. Everybody and his dog knows John Cooper." The hometown paper, the *Commonwealth* (now the daily *Commonwealth-Journal*)—with its editor, George Joplin, Jr., serving as campaign vice chairman—called Cooper's campaign "dignified" and added, "Judge Cooper understands people, speaks their language, is familiar with their problems and needs, and is supremely anxious to do something for Kentucky." But not even a majority of Kentucky Republicans voted for Cooper. He went down to defeat at the hands of one King Swope of Lexington.

But a broader call was in the making, a further step in the shaping of a global Kentuckian. American involvement in World War II was becoming inevitable. Japan's attack on Pearl Harbor, December 7, 1941, made it fact. A few months later, John Sherman Cooper enlisted in the army as a private, spurning a chance for an immediate commission as an officer.

Observing from the remoteness of rural Kentucky the ruthless spread of Hitlerism across Europe, Cooper had not been in line with the isolationist unconcern of many of his neighbors in Appalachia and, indeed, of many Americans elsewhere in the country. "In a strongly Republican family in a Republican county, I did not at first feel kindly toward Woodrow Wilson or internationalism," Cooper was to say later. "Then I began to read what he'd said." Even so, his tilt against isolationism was largely intuitive. It remained so until 1939 when he was called upon to deliver a speech in Lexington to the Kentucky Federation of Women's Clubs on the issue of isolationism versus intervention. Typically, Cooper spent three days at the University of Kentucky library boning up on Wilsonian concepts of foreign relations; as he once told a *Saturday Evening Post* interviewer, he thought he ended up giving a poor speech but the research clarified his conviction that the nation had a world-leadership responsibility. "I was deeply impressed with many of FDR's fireside chats to the nation on the subject," Cooper has recalled. "I followed the news of all of Hitler's moves and saw in motion pictures the crowd responses to his inflammatory speeches in places like Nuremberg—commanding, arousing, intense. I did not see how we could avoid reading this as an inevitable, fundamental threat to freedom and a sense of decency everywhere."

If barbarism could be halted only by military involvement, Cooper was among those who felt it was the proper course, and Pearl Harbor left no doubt of that. Cooper's stand should be considered in the light of the later years of the Cold War and of Vietnam when arch-conservatives in his party mistakenly thought him to be soft headed. To the contrary, he held to the Kentucky tradition that when there is no alternative to force, then fight like hell.

Cooper pinpointed his philosophy in Kentucky history terms when he made his 1948 speech to the Kentucky Society of New York.

"Kentuckians know that liberty under law and the institutions of a free government . . . must continually be preserved even if the struggle shall demand the sword," he said.

He spoke of how in early pioneer years, when 1,500 settlers were killed by Indians as they struggled to establish homes, 300 Kentuckians went with George Rogers Clark to Vincennes to win the West. In the War of 1812, a proud Cooper noted, 7,000 Kentucky volunteers were with Shelby and Johnson in Ohio and Michigan and her riflemen with their long rifles joined the Tennesseans in Andrew Jackson's victory at New Orleans. They were at the Alamo and at San Jacinto where Texas won her independence and where a flag made by Kentucky women was carried by Kentucky riflemen.

Said Cooper, "McKee, young Henry Clay, Jr., Jefferson Davis and Zachary Taylor are symbols of those who were at Monterey, Cerro Gordo and Buena Vista, and the villages in Kentucky which today bear Spanish names mark the return of the soldiers of the Mexican War. In the War Between the States, Kentucky furnished more troops to the North and South in proportion to its population than did any other state to either army.

"In the Spanish-American War it oversubscribed its quota of volunteers. In World War I it furnished the only county in the United States, Breathitt, where volunteers made unnecessary the draft; and in World War II, before selective service became effective, Kentucky gave a greater number of volunteers in proportion to its population than did any other state."

For Private Cooper, World War II led after basic training in 1942 to officer candidate school at Fort Custer, Michigan; he was graduated second highest in a class of 111 although he was its oldest member. He was assigned to the 15th Corps of General George Patton's Third Army as a courier in military police.

In the development of Cooper the diplomat and force in U.S. foreign affairs, his participation with the Third Army in the July 1944 entry into Europe and the Patton-led sweep across France, Luxembourg, and Germany proved less important than what came after.

Among the awful leavings of the war, Cooper saw the horrors of the Buchenwald concentration camp and throughout the war what he calls "the skinny people" of ravaged Europe. In Munich at war's end, on behalf of displaced persons threatened with being torn from their spouses and children for enforced shipment back to Russia, Cooper came face to face with—and stood up to—raw, inhumane communist power. By then an expert in military government in charge of the reestablishment of the judicial system in Bavaria, Cooper showed such an uncanny judgment that some of the unknown "non-Nazis" he chose as judges turned up later as leaders of a free West Germany.

The poor man's county judge from Pulaski County was on his way to a plateau of universal understanding.

3

JOHN COOPER'S WIFE, Lorraine, said the family does not think that the notoriously unpunctual Cooper ever wore a wristwatch until he was with Patton's Third Army in its spectacular World War II dash across Europe. "It was either a watch or be left behind," Mrs. Cooper said her husband sadly acknowledged.

Of his combat role Cooper has been reticent. "I was too old to be in combat, but in Patton's army you were always close," he says. He does recall that frequently he served as a messenger between Third Army field headquarters and divisional commands, traveling through the fluid battle zones by jeep. "It was interesting, and sometimes dangerous," he has said, mentioning in particular an episode on the Rhine near Remagen but never going into detail. "It was the young soldiers going forward, always forward, many soon to die, that brought home to me the tragedy of war."

Cooper, however, never has been reticent about General George Patton. He revered Patton. In 1950, as the speaker at the first reunion of Third Army veterans of World War II, Cooper said, "The soul of this Army was its leader. I cannot fix in words his restless spirit. By every standard he was one of the great combat leaders of all time. But he was more than that. His toughness, fearlessness, and daring inspired and gave pride to his men. He was proud of them."

In a 1974 interview Cooper reminisced about his personal experiences with Patton. "One day I saw him directing troop traffic at LeMans, France. It was rather a small town circle, reminding me of Somerset, and in the middle of it stood Patton shouting 'Move! Move!'" On another occasion when the Third's advance in France had been held up and troops were getting a respite around the city of Nancy, Cooper went to church and found Patton seated in a front-row pew and singing louder than anybody. At a party in Luxembourg after the Battle of the Bulge, there was an opportunity for a visit with Patton, during which Cooper says the general, "a great horseman," spoke fondly of Kentucky.

Cooper saw the Buchenwald concentration camp within a few hours after its liberation by the Third Army (Patton ordered the entire populace of nearby Weimar out to look at its horrors). Years later, Cooper's impressions retained all the shock of so many who shared that early view: "20,000 prisoners so weak they could hardly speak . . . the gas furnaces, and the bodies of victims racked up like bales of hay. I will never forget or forgive its inhumanity."

As a lieutenant and finally as a captain, Cooper remained in Germany until the end of 1945 performing duties far beyond the measure of his rank—and exercising in GI khaki the empathy he had displayed as a county judge. In addition to the reorganization of the Bavarian courts, he found himself serving as legal adviser to a colonel charged by the Third Army with repatriating 300,000 displaced war victims in Bavaria. There were Italians, Norwegians, Poles, French, and nationals of other countries, and some who claimed to be Americans among the throngs of homeless whom the Nazis had moved into Germany to do slave labor, Cooper remembered. "There were also thousands upon thousands of Russians."

Under terms agreed upon by the United States and the other allies at Yalta, all Russian nationals were to be repatriated—forcibly returned to the Soviet Union—

including those whose political views would bring them trouble in a communist homeland. "The Soviets wanted us only to feed them but not to allow them access to American literature or to let them see movies," Cooper said. He watched with growing concern as the Russian negotiators interpreted the Yalta agreements as meaning all Russians should be repatriated, but not their non-Russian spouses or children. He saw some of the Russian displaced persons being torn from their families and by force sent back behind what soon was to be branded by Winston Churchill as the "Iron Curtain." But the Supreme Allied Headquarters in London ordered compliance with the Russian interpretation.

"The World Council of Churches, the papal emissary, the Jewish agencies, they all registered complaints with Allied headquarters and at Munich they were referred to me," Cooper said. "I spoke to my immediate superior, Lt. Col. O. B. McEwan, now of Orlando, Florida, and he agreed to go with me to our superior officer who asked me, 'What right have you to question an order?' " The low-ranked Cooper's dogged response was that the policy was inhumane. "It will create a rightful furore in world opinion and particularly with public opinion in the United States," Cooper responded.

"All right, go see Patton if you want to, you have my permission," the colonel said. Cooper did just that. He and McEwan won an audience with Patton's executive officer who said, "I'm sure General Patton would agree," and immediately Patton rescinded the repatriation order in the Third Army occupation zone. "I've always been proud of that," Cooper said years later. "It meant the saving of thousands of family lives." He was cited for his action by the Third Army's military government section.

At the same time Cooper single-handedly was reorganizing for the military government the 239 courts in Bavaria, preventing Nazis from securing important posts and spotting as successors Germans who were qualified and genuinely non-Nazi. Kentucky acumen proved remarkable. One "skin and bones" man whom Cooper and fellow officer Lt. Col. George E. Rion recommended for a Bavarian government post as economic minister turned up years later as the portly figure at a White House reception. He was Ludwig Erhard, by then chancellor of West Germany, and when he again met Cooper, his greeting was, "Yes, I already know 'Captain' Cooper." Another Cooper recommendation in the shambles of Nazi defeat was Wilhelm Hoegner who had been forced to flee by Hitler but who became the first chief executive of Bavaria. Cooper's "friendly advice and quiet, unassuming authority" were qualities described in the citation that the Army awarded Cooper for his work at the time.

The influence of these experiences undoubtedly helped prepare Cooper for his quiet—yet as conservative fellow-Republicans and Democrats were soon to discover, nettlesomely independent—entry upon the national scene. Within a year, Cooper would be in the United States Senate. Thruston B. Morton, witty and world-minded Louisville Republican, who was himself destined to be a congressman, U.S. senator, and national party chairman, has said that Bavaria "created in John a perception of the sameness of human traits on both sides of the mountain." But before Washington began to feel the Cooper effect, there were two intermediate chapters to be played out: a brief term as a circuit judge—the highest trial court in Kentucky—and the campaign that surprisingly would give Cooper his first senate ticket.

He was still in Germany when Democrats joined Republicans to sponsor the army officer, now forty-four, as candidate for circuit court judge serving Pulaski and three neighboring counties. In July 1945 the *Louisville Courier-Journal* said editorially, "Lt. John S. Cooper, USN [*sic*], now with the Third Army in Europe, has the field in the 28th Judicial District. Mr. Cooper is a young man of good reputation and capacity, broadly educated, well-respected in his section and his state." His candidacy was unopposed.

Cooper went on the bench in January 1946 still wearing a GI shirt because white shirts were unavailable. He later told an interviewer that he spent lunch hours and nights boning up on the law and occasionally even recessed court in order to check some fine legal point. He felt that many of his rulings might be appealed simply on the basis of his absence from the law during the war years and he was anxious not to suffer any reversals and cause the needless delay and expense of appeals. The law was not to be treated carelessly, he said; under its protective shade lay the individual's refuge from misused power. While Cooper takes satisfaction from the fact that fifteen of his first sixteen decisions were affirmed by the Court of Appeals, another facet of that experience counts most: "I look back on my service because I was able to require in 1946 that black citizens be on both grand and trial juries." He accomplished this by ending the practice by appointed court commissioners of excluding blacks from the collection of names out of which jurors were randomly chosen.

Cooper served as circuit judge only a few months. Albert B. (Happy) Chandler had resigned his U.S. Senate seat two years short of its expiration to become national baseball commissioner. For John Sherman Cooper running for the Senate seemed an opportunity to involve himself in those human problems common to those on "both sides of the mountain." Cooper's Democratic opponent for the unexpired senate seat was popular John Young Brown, Sr. "John Cooper campaigned for that bobtail term as if he'd never heard that only two Republicans ever had been sent to the Senate by Kentucky through popular vote in all its history," says Morton, who simultaneously sought and won a house seat in 1946. "I never could quite bring myself to enjoy the exigencies of campaigning—but John had to touch everyone in the room, wherever he went."

As usual, Cooper's recollection is comically self-denigrating. He remembered the Democrat to whom he directed the normal greeting ("I'm John Cooper. I'm running for the Senate and I want you to vote for me") and extended a hand, to which the man responded reluctantly, "You're a Republican, h'ain't you?" When Cooper nodded yes, the man gave his hand with the comment, "Okay, just press it lightly."

Among the many who saw Cooper as a long-odds dark horse was Allan Trout of the *Louisville Courier-Journal*. Of the Cooper campaign, begun in a tent at Lancaster, Kentucky, Trout later told a colleague:

"My first impression was of his incredibly bad delivery. No polish, no flourish whatever. He searched for words, he mumbled, he seemed always to be preparing to apologize. But then I began noticing that he was having an almost hypnotic effect on the crowd. I couldn't figure it out.

"Then, in the courthouse in Richmond, I noticed those little old ladies, the kind who wear black velvet bands at their throats, sitting straight on the edge of their chairs as though they were at tea, and they were gazing at him with rapt faces. They weren't the type to turn out for a political rally, but they turned out for John Cooper.

"And then it dawned on me that his pained expression as he stumbled along, groping for words, seemed to say, 'I know I'm not much of a politician but I'm sincere. If you can't vote for me, at least feel sorry for me.' He was everything a politician is not, and they loved and trusted him for it. It's been his trademark."

Cooper won that 1946 race by a margin of 40,000 votes—a Republican record. It is agreed that few among his constituents knew that they were sending a "one worlder" to the Senate. Certainly few Kentucky Republicans knew it, nor did any senate Republicans in Washington.

"One thing I never thought of until recently," Thruston Morton mused in 1975, "is that regardless of party, senators and congressmen from Appalachia had pretty much been isolationists. Indeed, John Robsion, in the House from Louisville, was a *rabid* isolationist. Then here comes John Sherman Cooper on the Washington scene."

Cooper remembers with pride that one of his first actions upon taking his senate seat in 1947 was to co-sponsor legislation to allow emergency admittance to the United States each year for four years 100,000 persons displaced by Hitler. A Texas senator spoke of "subversives, revolutionists and crackpots," but Cooper said simply, "These are people who resisted and who will not return to a totalitarian state."

His maiden speech in the Senate was on January 22, 1947. It was in support of his vote against the transfer of the investigation of World War II graft and profiteering from the regular senate committee on executive expenditures to a special committee. This, Cooper felt, would turn the investigation into political hay-making. So his vote went against his party leadership's position. He was able to get his say in floor debate only by a grant of time from the Democratic side.

Just before Cooper spoke, Wisconsin's Senator McCarthy had played to the gallery. He suggested that failure to shift the war investigation to a special committee would be a message to "the wives and mothers of the 250,000 men who died during the war . . . the legless and sightless . . ." that wartime delinquencies would be left unprobed.

Cooper's cool statement was a forecast of many similar positions he would take in that body. The freshman senator saw no reason why the procedural rules needed abrogation. Not himself a member of the committee being challenged, his approach was on principle. He said that continuation of the probe by the regular committee would provide a needed expertise for future decisions in this area. And he concluded with a prescient statement which could be repeated now when illegalities by the

CIA and other executive agencies have come to light in the wake of the unveiling of the Watergate cover-up.

Said Cooper in that first senate speech, "It may be of no importance to any one except the present speaker, but it seems to me, speaking from the viewpoint of one coming recently from the outside, that one of the most disturbing factors we have seen during the past thirteen years has been the ignoring of rules of law, and sometimes an actual contempt of those rules, by some of those who were a part of the Government itself. For myself, I should like to uphold in this body, when I can, rules of law."

A quiet, stubborn force for decency consistent with the law and the rules had come to the Senate. When John Sherman Cooper again voted against the Republican party leadership, urging that the proceeds from the sale of surplus war material should be paid on war debts, it brought the late Senator Robert Taft up the aisle to ask the newcomer angrily, "Are you a Democrat or a Republican? When are you going to start voting with us?" Cooper answered mildly, "I was sent here to represent my constituents and I intend to vote as I think best."

Later on in that Republican-controlled Congress, acting Majority Leader Kenneth Wherry of Nebraska telephoned Cooper to try to bend him into line on another upcoming vote, with an appeal to party loyalty. As Cooper told a magazine interviewer, his quietly firm rebuttal to Wherry was, "You remind me of a basketball coach I had up at Yale. He used to talk just like you do before a big game. Maybe you're in the wrong business. We're not playing a game here."

A respect for what Taft soon perceived to be Cooper's motivations and painstaking thoroughness in coming to conclusions led the Ohioan to collaborate with the man from Somerset. Today Cooper looks back with pride on benchmarks of his first two senate years. With Taft, he and three others cosponsored the first bill for federal aid to education. It won senate approval but was not enacted into law until 1965. With fellow Kentuckian Alben

Barkley and Oregon's Wayne Morse, Cooper also put up a fight to end Jim Crowism in schools and public places and stood up for an end to contrived obstacles to voting rights for minority Americans. Later, over angry objections from physicians and others in Kentucky who were wondering how "left" Republican Cooper planned to go, he cosponsored Medicare. Cooper told a *Courier-Journal & Times Magazine* writer in 1972, "we had to try and I'm glad we did."

"When the Medicare bill was up, I got thousands of letters from back home, most of them against me. The doctors and the hospitals were against it. But I noticed that the old country doctors and the county officials—people who had been out in the country and had seen the plight of the people who live in the hollows and down the dirt roads—they were for it.

"And I remembered my experiences as county judge in Pulaski County, when I'd go out in the county and see these people—desperate, hungry, sick, and nowhere to turn, and no one to help them except the old country doctors. You just can't let people go hungry. You can't just let them lie there sick, to die. Not in this country. Not with all we've got."

Thruston Morton says after some years it got almost depressing to walk into one small town doctor's office and pharmacy after another and be greeted with "Oh, Morton, I'm a good friend of John Cooper's." One druggist in the Hart County town of Munfordville even proudly pointed out to Morton the toilet which Cooper had used one day after several hours of campaigning 'way back in 1939.

But it was in the area of America's role in the world that the 1947–1948 senate debut permitted him to stake his further claim. "It was a special opportunity to be on hand during the great debates that set the patterns for the defense and the economic rebuilding of Europe, so absolutely essential to our national security and economic well-being," Cooper says.

Some Republicans opposed the Marshall Plan, that

unprecedentedly massive and long-term program for the rejuvenation of war-stricken Europe, but not Cooper. He caught the eye and respect of Michigan's Republican Senator Arthur Vandenberg, the one-time isolationist who was participating with the Truman White House in the formulation of a bipartisan foreign policy. (Vandenberg preferred the term "un-partisan" according to *Time* magazine's John Steele, an editor of Vandenberg's papers.) As a newcomer, Cooper's immediate involvement with foreign policy was not very visible. Even so, Henry Cabot Lodge, then a Massachusetts senator, and a supporter of the Marshall Plan, remarked on Cooper's "vigorous and independent mind"; this led the *Louisville Times* to observe that perhaps no Massachusetts senator had ever said so much of a Kentucky statesman since Kentucky became a state. And why not? Behind that perennially knitted Cooper brow, under that usually uncombed, wavy, silvering hair, an intellect was weighing foreign policy problems and sifting them down to a final bargaining point as at a swappin' day in Pulaski County. At a time when Soviet expansion in Europe was the coiled spring against which American political leaders could whip up emotional public support for vast economic aid and a United States military presence on the continent, Cooper was saying rationally, of the Marshall Plan, "Its purpose is *not* to tell a nation it can't have communism if it votes for it, but rather to create economic conditions and insurance against external threat which will leave nations free to say *whether or not* they want communism."

At the 1948 GOP national convention Cooper supported Arthur Vandenberg even though politics might have dictated otherwise. Cooper was chairman of the delegation from Kentucky on which Thruston Morton also served. Contending with Vandenberg for the nomination were Thomas E. Dewey, Harold Stassen, and Robert Taft. In the end Dewey took the nomination.

"I'll never forget that convention," says Morton with

wry embarrassment. "I was Stassen's delegate man from the House (which shows you one of the things I later outgrew) and, unbelievably, Joe McCarthy was Stassen's senate man.

"But John Cooper's choice was Vandenberg—and John stuck with him to the end. He was firm in the belief that effective foreign policy equalled national survival and world peace and that no effective foreign policy was achievable without the bipartisanship Arthur Vandenberg had created."

Cooper headed toward the 1948 election in Kentucky and his first bid for his own full senate term with a record of having voted on the Republican side in the Senate only 51 percent of the time—lowest average of any GOP senator.

Cooper remembers with a boyish grin that his votes thwarting GOP majority hopes of overriding Truman vetoes led to his being linked in the press as a bloc with his new friend George Aiken, Republican Vermonter and dean of the Senate, and with those other mavericks, Wayne Morse of Oregon, Charles W. Tobey of New Hampshire, and William Langer of North Dakota. Among issues on which Cooper had parted from his party were GOP efforts to reduce funds for the Marshall Plan, a politicized investigation of the war, and industry-wide union-management bargaining. On the latter issue, he stood with Senator Taft.

In Kentucky politics, breaking from Republican ranks could have been counted shrewd. Indeed, Morton says one of Cooper's basic tenets was that no Republican in Kentucky could afford to become too partisan. What may have been shrewdness in others was for Cooper action in behalf of principle, as other 1948 actions suggested. Favoring tax cuts and opposing tax boosts always have been the best political medicine in Kentucky, but Cooper was one of only two Republican senators who supported President Truman against the early enactment of a tax cut. Cooper had fretted that such a cut might hamper "requirements and demands which may be made upon the country . . . to implement our international policy." Moreover, as he faced his 1948 election opponent, Democratic Congressman Virgil Chapman, Cooper had won some favor in the eyes of Kentucky labor—but refused to pledge a change in his support of the Taft-Hartley Act for all-out labor support.

Nor was it a popular move in Kentucky's nonurban sections when Cooper voted against limiting to a year the future extensions of the reciprocal trade act. He held out for giving the president and the Federal Tariff Commission longer range authority to decide when it was appropriate to include American items in trade agreements without danger to domestic producers. "Resolute refusal to associate himself with the footprints of the Republicans' dinosaur wing" was the description applied to Cooper's view of relaxing tariffs.

This came from the liberal, Democratic-leaning Bingham press in Louisville. The *Louisville Times,* which endorsed Morton for reelection to the House, also endorsed Cooper. In doing so, the paper spurned the recommendation of Senator Alben Barkley, then campaigning on the national Democratic ticket as Truman's running mate. "In two years, Kentucky's junior senator has been so conscientious, courageous and intelligent that it would obviously be a disservice to the state and nation to interrupt his career . . . ," said the *Times.* "Nothing Sen. Barkley has said convinces us that his Republican colleague should not be returned to Washington."

Presidential candidate Dewey visited Kentucky to say, "Whether you vote for me or not, will you do this, will you make me one promise? Will you vote for Cooper to go back to the U.S. Senate?"

Wayne Morse, then still a Republican, visited Louisville to pronounce Cooper the possessor of "one of the 10 most brilliant minds in the U.S. Senate" and to say "no man in the Senate has made a more favorable impression

41

during his short two-year stay than Cooper." Morse called upon labor to recognize Cooper as a man who could be counted upon to "exercise independence of judgment in protecting the rights of labor, employers and the public."

Morse rhetorically asked what constituents should want in a senator. "First, complete integrity. Cooper meets that test," Morse said. "Second, willingness to vote on issues in accordance with the facts as the senator finds the facts. Cooper has that willingness. Third, courage to rise above party regularity in the interests of the country when the senator believes his party is wrong. Cooper has demonstrated such courage and shown that he is no party yes-man. He has shown a deep devotion to the principles of constitutional liberalism."

This outside help proved of no avail. While Dewey lost Kentucky by 126,000 votes, Cooper came within 26,000 votes of his Democratic opponent but defeat was defeat. The trend at the top of the ticket was "more than ballot-scratching could overcome," the *Louisville Times* reckoned. Soon after the election, the wife of winner Chapman wrote Cooper to thank him for having run a clean campaign and having scorned the use of personal vilification.

Yet for Thruston Morton, election night 1948 stands as one index of Cooper's political acumen, to be manifested at a later time in vote-accounting in the Senate. "John probably couldn't keep his checkbook in balance, but he's had the damndest sense of political tides," Morton says. On that night in 1948, when early results showed Cooper had carried Jefferson County with the city of Louisville, Kentucky's most populous area, by 19,000 votes and Morton was about to congratulate him, the man from Somerset waved it off, saying "I have heard the vote from the First [Barkley's district]. Uh, uh—I won't win."

In January of 1949, having been rebuffed in his senate bid, Cooper entered private law practice in Washington.

But he was not to be long away from public life. At the urging of Senator Vandenberg, President Truman appointed him to represent the United States in the fall of 1949 as delegate to the United Nations General Assembly in replacement of John Foster Dulles. "I was very fortunate," Cooper says. "It was a time of great testing—and of much hope for the United Nations. Later on, of course, I would have to answer to Republican folks back home who would demand to know why I had accepted an appointment from Harry Truman."

It was to be the first of six key State Department assignments. The next year, Secretary of State Dean Acheson, whom Cooper had come to admire while observing him from the Senate, named the Kentuckian as his special assistant in the formation of the North Atlantic Treaty Organization. "There is no one else on whose loyalty and wisdom I would prefer to lean," Acheson said.

Events soon proved that, at the UN and among the foreign ministers and political leaders of Europe, the Acheson judgment about Cooper was correct. With a negotiator's sense, born of his home state tradition and political and judicial experience and refined as a senate independent, Cooper did not tromp on protocol for public show, yet found his way through it with quiet stubbornness to get things done. Where others foreswore further consultation, he boned up more and consulted further. He understood the Europeans' fear of Soviet aggression but brought sympathy to the question of why they seemed to be less than supercharged about preparation against the threatening possibility. Doubts were raised at home by partisan detractors, but he turned out to have the image and substance of what Europe expected an American ambassador to be.

4

ALTHOUGH LATER YEARS have shown Cooper's effectiveness in defending United States policies at the United Nations and in furthering the firm establishment of the North Atlantic Treaty Organization, at the time there were questions of his ability to deal with the incessant pressures brought to bear by the Soviet Union.

Cooper himself has readily acknowledged that dealing with the perils to peace and accommodating the essential needs of mankind are far more complex in the world of the 1970s than they were in 1950. The tension and strife engendered in the proliferating smaller nations have radically altered the problems which Soviet aggression and a truculent China posed for the United States and its allies twenty-five years ago. Speaking to his former Third Army comrades in August 1950, shortly after the invasion of South Korea by the communist forces of North Korea, Cooper made his own views clear. He singled out the threat of the Soviets to Europe and the West, pointing to their preponderant military strength of 80 divisions with 40,000 tanks and 19,000 planes available for action in Europe in comparison with the slightly more than 12 divisions maintained by the West and saying that this threat was the "greatest peril in history" to the United States and to Western Europe. The only choice for America was to help its allies achieve security through economic health and military deterrence. Beyond that was the intolerable option of nuclear warfare.

But some maintained doubts of his ability. One critic described him as "moral but vague." Indeed, Thruston Morton has noted that some found his speeches to lack incisiveness and wondered what he was talking about. And in the atmosphere of 1949–1950, with a Republican party badly fragmented on the issue of the nation's role in the world, some observers wondered if Truman's UN appointment of Cooper were mere "window dressing" for the purpose of defusing GOP opposition to the Truman foreign policy. Cooper recalls wryly, "It certainly didn't defuse [Indiana's] Bill Jenner, who wanted us to turn our backs on the world."

A cancer-stricken Senator Arthur Vandenberg had paid tribute to Cooper's "relentless loyalty to a sound bipartisan foreign policy for a united America." And within the limits of the modest national recognition given to Cooper's accomplishments (mostly because of his lack of self-promotion) the *New York Herald-Tribune* had noted that Cooper's UN appointment was "hailed by Democrats and Republicans alike." Even Senator Robert Taft applauded, although to him foreign policy bipartisanship was "a very dangerous fallacy threatening the very existence of the nation" because he thought it blunted what he felt should be "goading" of the White House and State Department by the political opposition.

As it turned out, Cooper won over the UN at the personal level. Soon, one minister from a member nation was pronouncing Cooper "among the most popular and able we have ever had." Nor did fuzziness of expression appear to impede Cooper's effectiveness. To the contrary, in an atmosphere of almost unbroken contentiousness, his down-home ability for making his points without invective was described as an ideal antidote for Russian fuming.

As he says, "There was complete disagreement on everything between the Soviet and western nations. I walked into denunciations and incessant Russian propaganda." But in his term as U.S. delegate and as alternate

45

delegate in three sessions of the General Assembly, he won added support for the United States by his manner of replying to strident Soviet polemics in his low-key halting way that highlighted their emptiness, and then outlining U.S. positions in what one observer called "iron mumbles." Cooper insisted upon expressing such positions in his own way, rather than in what he says was the stilted language and sometimes the logic of the State Department.

In October 1950, tart-tongued Andrei Vishinsky, leader of the Russian delegation, laid a bitter attack upon the administration of the Pacific Islands by the United States under UN trusteeship for being inimical to the islanders' determination of their own affairs. Vishinsky even charged it had led to widespread incidence of the yaws disease.

Cooper in answer first pointed out that U.S. policy in the islands already had been favorably covered in a UN report and therefore that Soviet elaboration in Assembly debate was superfluous. But, he then continued, "in order that the record may be set straight and to give point to my statement that mere denunciation is valueless and inaccurate, I will state briefly the facts on several points raised by the Soviet representative." He cited the number of self-governing "municipalities" already established on the far-flung islands (many of whose inhabitants voted to acquire U.S. commonwealth status in 1975). As for yaws, he noted that the "preliminary report" quoted by the Soviets as indicating a 90 percent incidence of the disease had in fact been an estimate by American medical authorities at the time U.S. trusteeship began; now, Cooper said, "yaws lesions were being found in less than one percent of islanders presenting themselves for treatment"—and the establishment of only ninety subdispensaries referred to scornfully by Vishinsky actually meant one clinic for every 600 inhabitants. Concluded Cooper: "It is the view of my delegation that emotion, bitter denunciation, or propaganda will not meet the issues . . . and, in fact, are a disservice to the people with whose welfare we are concerned."

Two months later, in December 1950, Cooper spoke to the General Assembly about the U.S. hopes for fail-safe international control and reduction of all armaments. This was a cause that would command his enduring participation all the way up to the SALT talks of the 1970s. One Cooper observer said smilingly he approached it in the way he dealt with Kentucky Democrats and heels-in-the-ground Republicans—lots of reasoning wrapped in earnestness.

On that December 1950 occasion, Russia's Vishinsky had responded to a disarmament plea, made by President Truman at the General Assembly, with one of those round-robin attacks against everything American. Delegate Cooper was chosen to respond. From Cooper it brought an evocation of his overriding sentiment that force brings misery.

Cooper began his rebuttal by reiterating Truman's basic principles of effective disarmament planning:

"First, the plan must include all kinds of weapons. Outlawing any particular kind of weapon is not enough. The conflict in Korea bears tragic witness to the fact that aggression, whatever the weapon used, brings destruction.

"Secondly, the plan must be based on unanimous agreement. A majority of the nations is not enough. No plan of disarmament can work unless it includes every nation having substantial armed forces. One-sided disarmament would be a sure invitation to aggression.

"Thirdly, the plan must be foolproof. Paper promises are not enough."

The United States, having pledged itself to the pursuit of a policy of cooperation in the UN and to maintaining peace by a system of collective security, had found it "easy" to decide to seek effective control with inspection of atomic energy and nuclear weaponry, Cooper said. He added, ". . . but the fact is inescapable that the Soviet leaders decided to forego effective international control. By 1948, the basic decision that the Soviet Union must have made had been recognized by the United Nations Atomic Energy Commission. That basic decision must have been that Soviet objectives and any real control of atomic weapons, or of disarmament, were mutually exclusive and incompatible."

Then Cooper turned to Vishinsky's diatribes: "I think it would be proper, as well as kinder to the General Assembly, if I were to accord the repetitious statements and arguments that we have heard from the representative of the U.S.S.R. their true significance—and not respond to them. Nevertheless, I think it is important that those who are less familiar with these specious proposals should have the record made clear."

Cooper noted that Vishinsky had "mentioned various individuals in the United States, dwelt at length upon our economic system and brought up matters which in his speech of over an hour contributed little to the real question [of international arms control].

"The true state of facts is that this subject has been under consideration for a number of years by a [UN] commission and a committee," to both of which the U.S.S.R. belongs. "Failure to reach agreement was the result of the lone position of the U.S.S.R.," Cooper said. "Therefore, if we find ourselves today without agreement, the record points to the cause."

As for Vishinsky's protests against what Cooper called "alleged U.S. threats to use the atom bomb" in the Korean conflict then being bitterly waged, the Kentuckian said, "I only have to say that no atom bomb has been dropped on Korea and, to the contrary, that the instruments of aggression have been those of great masses of men and of conventional weapons and tanks, as well as other new weapons of war, which are held in great quantity by the Soviet Union. All the talk in the world cannot alter that fundamental fact. If the Soviet Union had supported the United States plan for the control of atomic energy, the atom bomb would today be effectively banned and prohibited."

Cooper's performance begun in the autumn of 1949 at the UN brought from President Truman and Secretary of State Dean Acheson calls to other delicate assignments. Senate approval in 1949 of the North Atlantic Treaty had paved the way to U.S.-European military collaboration as a deterrent to Soviet aggression in Europe. But negotiations of the utmost skill were called for to make it effective. As Cooper later said in his 1950 speech to Third Army veterans, what was needed was the hard-headed organization of a common defense, a unified command under one leader, and the willingness of the European governments to match the commitment of U.S. troops with proportionate commitments of their own.

In April 1950 Cooper was sworn in as an ambassador-at-large to assist Acheson at the London conference of foreign ministers of the Atlantic Pact nations, meeting as a council to discuss defense organization. Later, in December, he was given an even bigger job: to work with the deputies of the various foreign ministers in helping put into effect the mutual defense decisions of the NATO nations. Then, for seven weeks Cooper remained in Europe at Acheson's request—as the Kentuckian recalls—exploring in a fact-finding tour the readiness of European governments to contribute their share to their own defense. He met with prime ministers, foreign and defense ministers, leaders of opposition parties, and national legislators, trade union leaders, businessmen, newspaper people, veterans, and students in seven of the NATO countries and western Germany, then under Allied occupation.

"What it meant was that John Cooper was present at 'the creation' " is the way it was assessed years afterward by William G. Miller, the young ex-Foreign Service man who became Cooper's foreign policy aide in the Senate during the years of antiballistic missile and Vietnam debate. "I think he did well because while he always asked severe questions, he never went for ad hominems. He had no intellectual blind spots, everything was open."

But Cooper says of that period, with a belittling shrug, "The Russian threat *really* threatened a weak people in Europe, so the European officials welcomed anybody who came from Truman and the American Secretary of State." He adds with a smile, "They appreciated the Marshall Plan assistance for their economic recovery but they also wanted a military force commitment from us—so they were very frank. They knew a U.S. force presence was the only sure deterrent against Soviet pressure or Soviet attack."

But in the United States such a commitment was quite another matter. Most leaders in Cooper's party were so opposed to troop commitments in Europe that when Acheson went to Brussels in December 1950, accompanied by a supportive Cooper, it was to the tune of GOP demands for the secretary's removal from office and lack of enthusiastic support by some Democratic leaders. "When we left that December day which was my future wife's birthday, Senator Alben Barkley was the only Democratic leader there to see us off," Cooper says.

"They do not mean to give aid, comfort and encouragement to the Communists, but these Republicans have been driven mad by their own partisan spleen" is the way the GOP attitude was described by the *Louisville Courier-Journal,* an irony considering how imminent was the period when Republican Senator Joseph McCarthy would be attacking Acheson as "the red Dean."

At the Brussels meeting, Cooper's earlier call for a unified NATO command was approved, with General Dwight Eisenhower as supreme commander.

Cooper did not flinch from meeting the issue within his party. In his August 1950 speech to his Third Army comrades, he stressed Europe's need to make its own sacrifices for adequate defense and to recognize that "you cannot have arms without tears." Cooper went on to say of U.S. commitments, "These decisions must be made quickly . . . are not the responsibility of the executive branch alone but of the Congress as well. . . . We stand in utmost peril. Interparty recrimination will not meet this danger. It must be met by action."

Somehow, the Cooper manner continued to turn aside vindictive riposte. Returning from the May 1950 London meeting with Acheson, Cooper had encountered Indiana Senator Jenner, one of the more strident of the GOP isolationists who were by mental gymnastics making anticommunism blend with opposition to U.S. troop commitments to NATO.

"I see you're representing the Republican Party over there in Europe," jibed Jenner over the fact that Cooper had made the mission as Acheson's "Republican" counselor.

"I doubt if I'm representing your views," Cooper responded.

"Well, I'd just as soon have you representing me as anyone I know," said Jenner, to Cooper's quiet satisfaction. It was the same kind of reaction to that "affidavit face" and intellectual approach as manifested some years afterward to Cooper's brother Don by J. Graham Brown, a feistily conservative Republican Louisville hotel man and financier. "I don't agree with one vote out of a hundred but I'm for that boy every time," Brown was to say.

Along with Cooper's successes during his UN and NATO assignments went his longtime habit of being as absentminded about personal details as he was meticulously unabsentminded about work and issues. This was detailed by the *Saturday Evening Post* in a 1954 profile on Cooper:

"Preparing for the NATO meetings in London in the spring of 1950, State Department planners who had experience with Cooper sent him a stream of messages reminding him to be sure to get vaccinated. To the surprise of no one, Cooper never got around to it. When the American delegation arrived in London, the British decided not to make an international incident of it. But on the British steamship voyage home . . . Acheson and others warned Cooper that he'd probably be interned at Ellis Island if he didn't get vaccinated, despite his diplomatic status.

"Cooper just went on looking preoccupied with something else. Finally, Acheson sought out the ship's doctor and asked for help. The doctor, who had a sense of humor, had formal invitations drawn up announcing that 'His Majesty's Ship' would stage a Cooper vaccination ceremony at four o'clock that afternoon.

"A pretty nurse was detailed to deliver an invitation to Cooper, take him by the hand and escort him to his own needling. When the semi-public vaccination was concluded, Cooper's fellow delegates broke into a cheer and then broke out the champagne to celebrate the event."

No forgetfulness, however, characterized Cooper's performance when he appeared as a witness in February 1951 before a joint Senate Armed Services and Foreign Relations Committee, chaired by the powerful Democrats, Senators Richard Russell of Georgia and Tom Connally of Texas. The committee was considering whether President Truman had power to send U.S. troops to Europe without congressional authority. Truman was opposed on both sides of the aisle, not only by isolationists but by those who like Dick Russell asserted the role of Congress.

Cooper drew upon his just completed seven-country consultations to rebut claims that U.S. help to Europe's defense would be of help only to a Europe which would not help itself. This no longer was a valid excuse. Europe's "will to fight" if necessary was there, Cooper said. Any doubt about U.S. purpose would ultimately encourage Soviet aggression or western European despair. He stressed that the proposal therefore was for the security of the United States.

President Truman's decision to send additional troops to Europe was "courageous and right," Cooper said. A decision by the Foreign Relations Committee, the Congress or the people forbidding or restricting the deployment of the troops could well be "the greatest surrender in history."

In retrospect, does not consistency dictate that the Cooper of the late sixties and early seventies, the Cooper who sought congressional limitations on use of presidential power in Laos and Cambodia, should have aligned himself in the fifties with his more resistant GOP compatriots? Shouldn't Cooper have opposed President Truman? (His green light from Congress for military backup of NATO included a limit on armed forces involvement that Truman promptly violated.)

After all, Harry Truman had made the decision to send United States forces into South Korea with UN sanction— but without congressional sanction (although most congressmen were supportive). It was a step which historian Arthur Schlesinger in *The Imperial Presidency* was to say "dramatically and dangerously enlarged the power of future Presidents to take the nation into major war." Now, for Europe in 1951, Truman and Acheson were saying it was within the power and duty of the president to send additional troops to Europe if he thought U.S. defense required it (and J. W. Fulbright and Wayne Morse were among those supporting the premise, at which they balked when Johnson and Nixon claimed such authority).

The record shows that Cooper rarely spoke of NATO without stressing its legality under the terms of the UN Charter. He was equally persistent in stressing the need for full support from the Congress for the implementation of all the NATO goals. An examination of his performance during the debates over policy in Southeast Asia suggests that even when he was leading Senate forces against military escalation he was chary of limiting a president's flexibility in military tight-pinches. Obviously, in 1951 he felt that the paramount issue was not presidential use of U.S. forces but their presence as a deterrent against the likelihood of aggressive war.

Yet in answer to the question whether his position on the presidential authority regarding U.S. forces in Vietnam were inconsistent, Cooper says, "It's a well-taken point. They *are* inconsistent. I can only argue that Europe was and is essential to American security—and Vietnam was not."

Cooper's 1951 fact-finding tour for Secretary Acheson, in any case, was "a tremendous opportunity" that left a deep and lasting impression. "Determine Europe's will to defend itself" is the way Cooper recalls Acheson's instructions. Among those with whom he conferred were Prime Minister Clement Atlee and Foreign Minister Aneurin Bevan of England, Winston Churchill, Sir Anthony Eden, and General Charles DeGaulle. John McCloy, United States High Commissioner for West Germany, took Cooper to dinner with Konrad Adenauer whom Cooper found "tall and big but not fat—a strong head and face—very considerate and very open in his conversation." Cooper also conferred with Willy Brandt—"Brahnt" in Cooper's pronunciation—later the heroic mayor of encircled West Berlin. "He was unusually happy to talk, capable and a good politician who, like an American politician, gave you a Liberty Bell to take away."

Indeed, the German facet of the 1951 tour seemed to have impressed Cooper most deeply of all in personal terms. It was a return to the area he had seen in World War II where Hitler's victimization of the Jewish people and of thousands of forced laborers had so moved the Kentuckian.

"There I talked to a larger number of people than in any other country," he told the Senate Foreign Relations Committee. "I am certain that Western Germans have made their choice with the West. Eight million expellees and hundreds of thousands of veterans who were prisoners of the Russians know their cruelty and tyranny. But the Germans are exposed. They will not arm before there is some assurance of security. They do not believe there will be such assurance without United States participation in defense."

That assurance was given, of course. The emergence of NATO effectiveness was what caused Cooper's role to be regarded by some at the time as equal in the political realm of NATO to that of General Eisenhower in the military sphere. For Cooper, it generated a healthy disavowal of cliché images of America's career officials in the world of diplomacy, in which he had proved himself as acceptable as on Troublesome Creek or in Glasgow, Kentucky. "For most of them [in the Foreign Service]" he said later, "politics is out, they work hard, and it is not fair to look on them in the striped pants-cocktail party image. I admire them."

But it was time for Cooper to resume his mainstream ambition: the U.S. Senate. After less than four years' service Virgil Chapman, victor over Cooper in 1948, was dead in 1952, and yet another two-year unexpired senate vacancy beckoned. It was the year of Eisenhower versus Adlai Stevenson.

5

WHEN COOPER took to the hustings in 1952 seeking Chapman's unexpired senate seat, he found himself pinched by an awkward political dilemma in his Kentucky, nominally three to one Democratic.

He had been serving the nation with distinction in the United Nations and in Europe. But he had been doing this as an agent of a Democratic president and a Democratic secretary of state. Now, as a Republican, Cooper was running on the ticket with Dwight Eisenhower and Richard Nixon who were hitting hard at the Truman administration for a corrupting cronyism and a failure to win or end the Korean War.

"I knew there was resentment at home over my having taken an appointment from President Truman," Cooper recalled. "After my defeat in 1948 I'd refused at least two bipartisan spots on commissions because the folks at home might think I was just looking out for myself.

"But the United Nations and NATO assignments were something else. They were a national duty."

He remembers how the resentment surfaced at a campaign rally before a big crowd in Ashland, Kentucky, in May 1952. A voice from the audience demanded bitterly, "Why'd you, a Republican, take an appointment from Harry Truman?" As Cooper remembers it, "I said it was because I'd do anything to prevent another war. I believe I stretched my arms out. And, do you know, they cheered me!"

But he was counted strictly an underdog. His opponent was former Representative Thomas R. Underwood, editor of the *Lexington Herald* in Kentucky's Bluegrass country and the interim appointee for the senate vacancy. Among many of his own potential supporters in Kentucky Republicanism, Cooper was a suspect liberal internationalist—as one GOP Baptist from Kentucky's Scott County was wont to say of him, "a fine name but very little religion and no reliable politics at all."

Time magazine took note that Eisenhower, campaigning in Louisville, totally forgot to mention Cooper until after sitting down and then jumped back to the microphone to make a perfunctory endorsement.

Even the support of the liberal Louisville press was denied Cooper. In 1950, during his service in the UN and with NATO the *Louisville Courier-Journal* and the *Louisville Times* had said editorially that it would be a loss to the nation if rumors of Cooper's standing for governor proved true and he were to seek a state office. Better to wait until 1954 and run again for the Senate, the editorials admonished. Cooper did not run that year for governor.

But after Chapman's death in 1952, when Cooper did run for the Senate, the papers reneged. Owned by Barry Bingham, Sr., then active in the Stevenson campaign, they feared the prediction from Thruston Morton, Cooper's campaign manager, that a Cooper victory would mean the GOP could organize the Senate. This, said the newspapers worriedly, would place extremist GOP isolationists and reactionaries in key committee chairmanships. Moreover, the papers said, Cooper appeared in his campaign utterances to have "drifted from his old moorings."

"His opening speech contained a statement on foreign policy that might have fallen from the lips of any unenlightened isolationist working out of Republican campaign headquarters. All of Cooper's foreign experience seemed to tell for nothing. He dealt only in condemnation. . . . The war must be won quickly in Korea, but without risk. We must guard our interests more fully throughout the world, but spend less money to do it. We must, in short, elect the Republicans and let them utter a magic spell that will freeze Joe Stalin in his tracks."

Later, the newspapers asserted that Cooper, as a man who had committed "the unpardonable sin of being a liberal Republican in the 80th [1948] Congress," had to make his peace with those in control of Kentucky's GOP organization; yet his seeming praise now of those "reactionary Old Guard Republicans" whom he had blamed for GOP candidate defeats in 1948 "fall strangely from his lips." After "mature deliberation," the Louisville papers were endorsing Cooper's opponent. Editor-publisher Bingham said years later, "There is no question Cooper was the superior of the two candidates as a human being. The trouble was the party company he had to keep, and the obeisance he had to make to party regularity at election times."

Yet in the end the man with the listening ear and the earnest handshake prevailed, where party anachronisms and press defections did not. On election night, after assessing the early returns, Cooper turned to Thruston Morton, his campaign manager, and said quietly, "We've won."

In his own Republican district, he ran far behind Eisenhower-Nixon. But elsewhere, many Stevenson Democrats split their tickets to support Cooper. While Eisenhower lost Kentucky by 700 votes, Cooper won it by a solid 29,000. And he had won it cleanly. There is the story of the supporter who had proposed to Cooper that he make points against the Democrats by blasting them for the syndicate-linked gambling and scandals that had been exposed in the northern Kentucky cities of Covington and Newport. "What's that got to do with the national issues?" Cooper had said, rejecting the notion.

The Louisville papers proved correct in some of their fears of Old Guard Republicans taking over major senate committee chairmanships. But what Cooper did in the Senate in 1953 and 1954 demonstrated that, far from drifting from his old moorings, he maintained his usual independence.

Move by move, he was resuming his course toward becoming what his colleagues often characterized as the conscience of the Senate—standing alone, or at least apart from colleagues of either party on many critical issues, yet drawing respect from many with whom he disagreed. Senator Paul Douglas of Illinois called him "the noblest Roman of the Senate." It was nothing Cooper cared to flaunt but toward the close of 1953 the left-leaning Americans for Democratic Action named him the Senate's "most liberal" Republican.

The following year, 1954, when Cooper faced former Vice President Alben Barkley in a race for what could be his first full term, it was to Kentucky that President Eisenhower made his first trip of the political season—a contrast to that 1952 race when Eisenhower forgot even to mention Cooper's name. This time, Eisenhower was told that in the eyes of the nation's press Cooper was the prototypical "Eisenhower Republican."

Accomplishments in domestic as well as foreign legislation led to this belated recognition. For his Kentucky constituency Cooper won, in the 1953–1954 session, extension of 90 percent parity price supports of tobacco, which he had initiated in 1948. As a member of the Labor Committee, he offered influential amendments and backing for changes in the Taft-Hartley Act recognized as desirable both by labor and management. He had initiated, in the Republican-controlled Senate, flood control for Kentucky rivers and the development of the Ohio River and had supported TVA and rural electrification. But it was in the context of sterner controversies, involving the nation's constitutional and moral approach to its stance in the world, where Cooper applied his distinctive combination of heritage, methodical study, and opposition without rancor. The controversies brought him

59

into differences with his GOP colleagues and, on occasion, with his president.

One such instance of alignment against most party colleagues was the year-long national debate over the attempt by Ohio's Republican Senator John Bricker to secure a constitutional amendment curbing the treaty-making powers of the president. Cooper concluded after study that nothing like the compelling forces needed to warrant tampering with the nation's basic code existed in this situation. On all six key roll-call votes in the Senate on the Bricker resolution, Cooper was the only Republican to vote "no." The speech he made in opposition to the proposal was judged by the nation's press as the most influential from Republican senate ranks where doubting remarks about the resolution were not altering votes. Bricker had the names of seventy senators from both parties on his resolution. But after Cooper had finished his speech, Barry Goldwater who was presiding told Cooper, "You almost convinced me!" Says Cooper, "I can't brag on it too much, but Bricker did lose enough of his support for the resolution to be defeated."

Cooper began that speech by suggesting that, like many Americans, he had found the question complex and difficult to understand. He paid tribute to Senator Bricker for "the ability and patriotic sincerity" which had led the conservative Ohioan to "bring the important subject of the treaty-making power to the attention of the Congress and the country." Then, in twenty pages of text reflecting careful historical and legal research, Cooper set forth the evidence behind his reasons for opposing the amendment. There were echoes in his pronouncement (although emphatically not in the manner of delivery) of intellectual Kentucky forbears, notably Henry Clay. Among Cooper's major points were:

"The Constitution is our basic natural instrument of government and ought not to be amended unless the most persuasive reasons for change can be established.

"The purpose of the Bricker resolution was not to

preserve but to make far-reaching changes in the Constitution that had served so well, as of then, for 165 years.

"The President and the Senate have not ratified any treaty with which I am familiar which has cut across the rights and interests of our people," Cooper concluded. ". . . the Constitution provides safeguards against treaties which may be unwisely negotiated and we must believe that future Presidents and members of the Senate will be as jealous of the Constitution and individual rights as those who form our Government today.

"We should not try to impose upon those who will live in the future limitations which have not been imposed on American citizens during the last 165 years. If in the future new conditions arise which demand change, it will be their day of decision."

Threatened infringements on individual rights produced Cooper's greatest uneasiness in 1953 and 1954. Especially the rights of those put upon or hard beset, the people up the dirt roads and in the mountain hollows, the blacks and their millions of counterparts elsewhere in the nation and the world; Cooper's thinking linked them, and he felt the party of Lincoln should have its closest ties with them. By the same token, he stewed over what he felt were violations of the rights of other Americans, provoked in the course of blunderbuss congressional investigation of the American communist movement. The senator spotted a pattern of "witnesses being encouraged to lie in order to save their own skins." When Cooper saw statesmen and intellectuals being pilloried for past beliefs or casual associations now carelessly labeled as treason, he put it in the same category of injustice as poor people denied basic access to the justice system or the rights of the ballot or of labor organization for purpose of protest.

Wisconsin's Senator Joseph McCarthy had been riding high with his flamboyant persecution of suspected communists. At one point, this produced a round of international name-calling. McCarthy suggested that Winston

Churchill was weak on communism. As the *New York Times* noted, Cooper was the only senator to take the floor to challenge McCarthy and defend Churchill.

In 1954, Cooper commanded attention with what *Commonweal* magazine later called "an altogether remarkable address" to a civil liberties conference on the subject of congressional investigations.

"Party divisions can be corrected," he concluded on that occasion. "There can be relatively swift enactments of programs to reinforce our capacity to meet external threats or the threat of subversion at home.

"But the larger danger is not so easily corrected. It is the damage done to the very institutions of government by which sound programs are devised, and the damage done to the concept of human rights which all our institutions are designed to serve. All of us want to protect in every way our system of free government from external attack, or from subversions within. But we want also to protect always the free structure of government itself. Without the protection of individual rights and freedom, our system will have little light and meaning."

Cooper had memories of Kentucky moonshiners he had freed because they had been brought into his court on the basis of illegally seized evidence. Such memories helped him oppose moves to allow illegal wiretap evidence in federal courts and to reduce Fifth Amendment rights against self-incrimination by witnesses before committees of the McCarthy ilk and in the courts. In 1968, Cooper was one of only four senators who voted against the Omnibus Crime Bill, on the grounds which he noted in senate debate that its wiretapping provisions and related elements were unconstitutional, invading the Fifth Amendment rights of individuals. Subsequently, the Supreme Court did judge a part of the bill's wiretapping provisions unconstitutional.

Yet when it came time for the Senate to consider stripping McCarthy of his major committee chairmanship, it was Cooper who—while noting that McCarthy

John Sherman Cooper, after Graduation from Yale, 1923

In Senate Office, Washington, 1958   Courtesy of Tom Abello

had extended and abused his great powers—nonetheless urged his colleagues to steer clear of the same excesses. It was a revealing evocation of his 1947 debut speech. It was as if he were back home asking Kentuckians to eschew rancor in favor of rational discussion. It was the judge calling for a return to reason.

"I have never voted for any motion or actions I thought in contradiction of the spirit of law or orderly government," Cooper said. ". . . In all the controversy about the junior senator from Wisconsin during the last two years, I have never made a denunciatory statement about him. . . .

"One of the reasons I would not do so is that in the last 20 years there has developed in this country the practice of denunciation of people who did not happen to agree with the views of those who are in power. Many of those who bitterly oppose Senator McCarthy call for the same [extra-legal] tactics that they charge him with."

The nation, cautioned John Sherman Cooper, should be wary of the plea of "emergency" as a pretext for the excessive use of power by anyone in any cause. This, he said, had brought on Franklin Roosevelt's scheme to "pack" the Supreme Court, the expulsion of American citizens of Japanese descent from their homes on the west coast during World War II, the 1945 proposal that Uncle Sam draft striking workers into the army, and, under Harry Truman, federal seizure of the steel mills. Once again, Cooper had put acrimonious dispute into conceptual framework. He did not stop with that issue.

He was in the vanguard of those who fought President Eisenhower to a standstill on the almost scandalously dubious Dixon-Yates contract that would have eviscerated TVA, then still a Godsend to the region of which Kentucky is a part. In a senate speech he proposed that, instead, TVA be authorized its own bonds for capital outlays. Later Cooper's suggestion became law. He voted against his party's attempt to deprive New Mexico's Democratic Senator Dennis Chavez of his seat because of

63

alleged election fraud and against the giveaway of tidelands oil leases; he was among the first to oppose White House appointment of Albert Cole, an open opponent of public housing, as Federal Housing Administrator. Alone among senate Republicans, Cooper fought the Eisenhower administration's Mexican Farm Labor bill which, in the absence of agreement between the two countries on migrant worker policy, authorized U.S. recruitment of Mexicans for work in American fields at a substandard rate of pay.

Meanwhile, early in May 1954, besieged French forces gave up their last-ditch stand in a fort at Dien Bien Phu, and there was communist victory in Indochina. Senator Lyndon B. Johnson of Texas was among those attacking Secretary of State John Foster Dulles and the Eisenhower White House for soft, inadequate policies that he charged had failed to stave off a disaster.

In a speech on the day that brought the surrender news, Cooper did not manifest prescience about the morass that subsequent years would bring because of the U.S. view of conditions in Southeast Asia. Indeed, while strongly commending the Eisenhower-Dulles efforts to unite European allies and free Asian nations in some bolstering diplomatic support of the French cause, Cooper said, "If they [the administration] had decided that stronger military steps should be taken I would have supported them, [and if they] so decide in the future, I will support them."

Cooper voiced no doubts about the U.S. stake. The French, together with the help of Vietnamese and Laotians had been engaged in "a fight for freedom."

"Today we are confronted with the same problem which we faced in Korea and China, whether it is possible to devise measures in concert with other nations which can prevent the loss of Indochina and other Asian states, vital to the security of the United States and to the freedom of the world," Cooper said.

Yet in his impromptu remarks that day, Cooper took a

strong stand in favor of negotiation; he did so even while defending the administration for its having raised Secretary of State Dulles' "massive retaliation" as a considered option.

"It seems to me that it was perfectly natural and proper to have suggested every possible alternative for action. . . . But it must not be forgotten that a great and continuing effort was made and is now being made to find a basis for collective action which will make unnecessary the use of these alternatives," Cooper said.

"It is suggested now that it may be possible through negotiation to find a basis of settlement in Indochina. Considering that our alternatives are losing Indochina entirely, or war with the entry of our troops, I believe that the choice of negotiation may be the only possible choice available to us. If it can be accomplished without the compromise of freedom, we should pursue it. . . . It may well be that the Congress itself has limited the choices which could have been made, by its speeches against negotiations—its insistence upon conformity with its policies.

"The effort of the administration to find a basis for collective action by our allies to prevent either the loss of Indochina or intervention of American military forces was the only course available." In retrospect, Cooper deems it important to recall that Eisenhower did refuse to intervene by force in Indochina.

However, neither statesmanlike utterances, willingness to buck his party when he thought its policy wrong nor courageous stands for individual rights availed Cooper in 1954. His opponent for the senate seat was former Vice President Alben Barkley—a grizzled seventy-six but Mr. Democrat in Kentucky—tale-spinning, young-wifed, a more colorful natural than Cooper for family reunions and election rallies.

Cooper pinned his hopes, in part, on attracting the votes of women and blacks for his stands on peace and civil rights issues. In what he says was the most vigorous campaign of his life, Cooper visited all of the state's 120 counties, made more than 150 speeches, drew supportive appearances from Vice President Richard Nixon and Senator Everett Dirksen as well as from President Eisenhower. Inasmuch as Barkley also was able, experienced, and an internationalist, Cooper recalls "we had trouble finding issues." The chief thrust of the Cooper campaign was that he was preferable as being less a strict party man, willing as he suggested Barkley never was to let "issues and the special problems of people" transcend party regularity.

Cooper's sister, Fostine, said, "He worked so hard—but he wouldn't permit the use of rumored contract scandals as ammunition against Barkley. Even so, John carried the smart places, damn it! He carried Louisville—and Lexington, and our District."

But it was Barkley's game. Once again, Cooper, now fifty-three, had failed to win a full senate term. His political career appeared at an end.

His ally, Thruston Morton, by then an assistant secretary of state, was in Spain on election day and received the bad news there. Upon his return to Washington, he telephoned Cooper to ask what the now lame-duck senator wanted by way of job consideration from the Eisenhower administration. "Typically, John replied 'nothing,'" Morton remembers. "But then, around the cocktail party circuit, I learned that John was really hurt that the administration had not asked him about his future interests." Morton went to see Secretary of State Dulles about making amends. "The ambassadorship to India would be a natural for Cooper. He'd really get out with the people," Morton quotes Dulles. But there remained the hurdle of President Eisenhower.

"When we went to see him, Eisenhower said, 'Foster, this sonuvagun Cooper bucked me on A, B and C,' and he ticked off issues where John had voted against the administration." But in the end the president saw the wisdom of the India idea and relented, Morton says. However, in a subsequent conference between Morton and Dulles, the secretary of state told Morton, "Nobody should be our ambassador in India without a hostess. I hear John Cooper has been seeing a lot of Lorraine Shevlin."

Lorraine Rowan McAdoo Shevlin was a well-educated, unusually charming "grass widow," often described by the Washington press as "a capital socialite." If the social gatherings at her red-brick, Federal home on N Street in fashionable Georgetown were not as newsy as those thrown by such other more publicized hostesses as Perle Mesta and Gwen Cafritz, they were at least as admired in inner circles for their graciousness and the quality of their conversation.

Mrs. Shevlin was the daughter of a wealthy Los Angeles businessman, educated at select private schools in Maryland, France, and Italy where her mother had been remarried to a Vatican official, Prince Domenico Orsini. Mrs. Shevlin's first marriage was to Robert McAdoo, son of William Gibbs McAdoo, who was Treasury secretary under Woodrow Wilson and later a United States senator from California. A second marriage, ended by divorce, was to Tom Shevlin, Jr., sometimes described as "a Palm Beach playboy."

During World War II, Mrs. Shevlin had worked as a volunteer for the Commission on Inter-American Affairs, headed by Nelson Rockefeller. As a quick-study linguist who added self-taught Russian to her command of French, Italian, and Spanish, she had been sent by Rockefeller to the 1945 UN charter assembly in San Francisco.

Thruston Morton recalls that it was he who first arranged the formal introduction between Mrs. Shevlin and Cooper, one of Washington's most eligible bachelors. Cooper did not have that status in 1947 when he first moved to Washington. In 1943 he had married Evelyn Pfaff, an army nurse; the move to Washington ruptured what apparently never had been a successful union and the marriage ended in divorce. As a bachelor Washingtonian, Cooper lived in the Dodge House Hotel and used the elegant Cosmos Club to entertain, but worked eleven-hour days and limited himself to two nights out a week. Mrs. Shevlin actually had first met Cooper at a 1948 party, when—betraying a somewhat imperfect grasp of agriculture—she asked for openers, "Senator Cooper, how is the burley cotton crop doing in Kentucky this year?" As she later recalled, "He gave me a queer look. I didn't see him again for two years."

She was cool, aristocratic, sophisticated; he was what columnist Drew Pearson had called "homespun." As a girl she had read and been charmed by "The Little Colonel" books, the gentle classics set in rustic Pewee Valley outside Louisville and later turned into a movie vehicle for Shirley Temple. "Little did I think Kentucky one day would become my adopted state," Mrs. Cooper said. One of her Washington friends was Jacqueline Bouvier, then dating Jack Kennedy, recently elevated from the House to the Senate. "We used to lunch together and say how awful it must be to be married to a man in politics."

John Cooper and Lorraine Shevlin had, indeed, become a frequent pair by that day early in 1955 when the secretary of state inquired of Morton if relationships were such that Lorraine Shevlin might be a prospect for consort to a U.S. ambassador to India. "I've known her a longer time than you," Dulles said, when Morton began to describe her aptitudes. "Thruston, you bring Ccoper in here tomorrow at 10." Says Morton: "Next day, Dulles said to John, 'I understand you're crazy about her and she's crazy about you. Why don't you get married?' "

This exercise in diplomatic prodding produced a $5 loss for Morton, who bet Representative John Robsion that Cooper would take the same, sometimes maddeningly long time to make up his mind about marriage that colleagues had found him taking with senate issues. But as New Jersey's Senator Clifford Case was to say almost twenty years later: "We know that when he reaches a decision, it is [one] that is worth waiting for."

As it turned out, the ambassadorship was a key. Cooper told a Louisville interviewer long afterward that marriage had been put off because he had doubts about moving into Mrs. Shevlin's handsome home—"mountain pride, I guess." With India in immediate prospect, "we didn't have to move into her house or mine, but into the embassy, and by the time we came home that sort of thing had solved itself."

When Cooper appeared before the Senate Foreign Relations Committee for confirmation of his appointment, his senate successor Alben Barkley accompanied a hearty "aye" with the comment, "I'm glad to say that I did John a good turn, though he may not appreciate it. I beat him and now he is going to have a very interesting position. And, second, he is going to marry that nice girl I've been trying to get him to marry for the past two years."

Cooper's swearing-in as ambassador to the world's largest (and, in Cold War terms, most maddeningly neutralist) democracy was followed immediately by the couple's wedding in the bride's native California and their departure for New Delhi. Secretary Dulles called the assignment "of utmost importance to the peace of the world." U.S. News and World Report hoped Cooper's "persuasive ways" would work in "a key Cold War spot—one of the most difficult and delicate in all the diplomatic world." Thruston Morton, who had played such a prime role, said it was as if John Sherman Cooper were off to cement relations with an Appalachia of 500 million.

6

FROM THE BEGINNING of India's independence in 1947, it was in America's interest to see that this largest of Asian democracies should survive and, as a country with acute economic problems, not be driven into communist embrace.

But by 1955 relations between the two nations were sorely strained. Many influential U.S. politicians and some press voices were calling the neutralist policies of Prime Minister Jawaharlal Nehru a charade favoring the communist cause. Considering the $200 million in U.S. aid already granted India, some demanded, what was Nehru up to visiting Chou En-Lai in Peking? Where was the gratitude?

Even Chester Bowles, U.S. ambassador to India in 1951–1952, conceded in a 1954 book, "Nehru fights communism in India but underestimates its dangers to the world." Yet Bowles deplored what he saw "with profound regret and misgivings" as a serious decline in Indo-American understanding. And he warned, "What Nehru says, most free Asians think"—adding, "The history of our time will hereafter be written largely in Asia."

Nehru's enigmatic brilliance and his belief that the United States maintained an economic imperialism matching Russia's revolutionary imperialism did not help allay widespread American fears about India.

John Kenneth Galbraith, Harvard University's retired

economics eminence, social analyst, and premier campus ego, once remarked of India that one of its shahs was building the Taj Mahal when the Pilgrims were building log cabins in Salem. But such ancient developments had been of no benefit to the masses. Widespread illiteracy, unchecked population growth, a primitive economy, and an average per capita income of well under $100 a year characterized the hundreds of millions of people who astonishingly accepted the way of political democracy after World War II.

It was Nehru's view that the only way to make political democracy work in teeming, impoverished India was through economic socialism. In his judgment there was a second condition—wire-walking nonalignment in the gigantic power struggle between the United States and the Soviet Union. Nehru also felt it vital to maintain maneuverability toward potential enemies, neighbor Pakistan nearing conflict with India over the strategic state of Kashmir and behemoth China.

But before his visit to Peking, Nehru had strongly opposed the U.S. military response in Korea and had been against China's being branded an aggressor in the United Nations for its role in Korea. Nehru also favored the return of Formosa to mainland China. And the strident anti-American outbursts of Krishna Menon, India's chief spokesman in the UN, made more difficult a reasoned examination in the United States of the extent to which these policies by India were part of her game plan for survival.

They certainly did not persuade John Foster Dulles, President Eisenhower's secretary of state, to whom anything less than undeviating allegiance to the U.S. side in the Cold War tended to suggest a tilt to the enemy side. Dulles' intentions to arm Pakistan worsened the situation. Early in 1955, when delegates from the remotest reaches of Asia and Africa attended a conference in Bandung, Indonesia, Nehru played a leading role as a spokesman for "Asia for Asiatics," but in such Dulles-

71

supporting, influential elements of the American press as *Time* and *Life* Nehru was pictured as an exponent of anti-Americanism.

This was the boiling kettle into which John Sherman Cooper moved in the spring of 1955. A yardstick of how he functioned was provided later by Professor Galbraith, a visitor to New Delhi while Cooper was there and himself dispatched as ambassador to India and Nepal by President Kennedy in 1961. Wrote Galbraith that year: "Cooper had become the American for whom, next perhaps only to Mrs. [John F.] Kennedy, Prime Minister Nehru entertained the greatest affection."

Galbraith should have included Lorraine Cooper in his pantheon, for it became quickly clear that a strong diplomatic team had been formed.

"It was protocol, protocol, protocol," Cooper remembers. "Between the hangover of British tradition and the newness of the nation, all the rituals were observed." He adds, "I never knew about such stuff"—implying that it was a breeze for his new wife.

For example, a testing highlight during the 1955–1956 Cooper ambassadorship was the visit to India of Russia's then-President Nicolai Bulganin and Communist Party leader Nikita Khruschev. "Wherever they went in India they campaigned, they gave the United States the devil," Cooper winces. "It was fascinating to see how well they'd prepared, for they played on every Indian problem, they touched on every one of India's sensitivities against the United States. It was for me a valuable lesson in the careful and thorough preparation and appropriate propaganda of the Soviet Union, which must be continuously watched by the U.S."

But at Prime Minister Nehru's gala diplomatic reception, when the Russians were ushered down the receiving line and came to Lorraine Cooper, she responded in Russian. "Nikita jumped!" Cooper recalls joyfully, still savoring the experience. He explains admiringly that she had studied Russian while working with emigrés during World War II and had done voluntary translation work for the State Department. "Some people are linguists. I studied German in high school, French at Yale," Cooper says, "but they and I never quite understood each other."

On another occasion early in the Coopers' India tour, when the Czechoslovakian ambassador called on them and brought an interpreter, Mrs. Cooper said to him in Russian, "Why don't we speak Russian, Excellency? It would be so much cozier."

It is no surprise that even now some Kentuckians, unaware of Cooper's earlier accomplishments abroad, believe that the key to success in India was Lorraine Cooper. Such notions reckon without Cooper's combination of simple likability and sensitive finesse.

He demonstrated this on one of the first occasions when he was summoned to confer with Nehru. "It was one day while his parliament was in session," Cooper says with his customary way of making the insightful appear commonplace. "I talked for about five minutes, but then I said I could see he was busy and I suggested some other time. He gratefully agreed. Next day I got a call to come to his home at 9 p.m. for what proved to be a most useful and informative visit because it was relaxed." After that, Cooper says, it became a custom for the two to meet at night at Nehru's residence, sometimes as late as 9:30. "I learned that then he would talk openly about India's relations—with the U.S., the Soviet Union, and China."

In Washington, Cooper already had attracted notice for the way he always had time for elevator operators, doorkeepers, and train conductors—sometimes because they had been understanding of his missing his floor or getting on a train without a ticket. Now he continued his interest in people in New Delhi.

"He was endlessly inviting people to the residence," Mrs. Cooper remembers. "It was challenging to an orderly person like me who ran the house. For a party, I had always insisted upon something decent to eat, plus a thought-out reason to be together because that's when you really learn.

"What seemed especially asinine at first was John's constantly asking me to receive Indian school groups. A high school class from Madras. A clutch of youngsters from Bangalore. It meant an endless chain of lemonade and brownies—the only American cookies India knew how to make.

"Why did they want to meet us? Why these young people? I soon learned. Maybe they weren't doing much in international diplomacy—but they wanted to see the live resident in the house of a country they'd heard so much about."

It was an especially parlous time for Indo-U.S. relationships—apparently well suited for Cooper's quiet candor in official discussions and his indisposition to make headlines in either country just for the sake of publicity. "John rarely gave interviews while ambassador," Mrs. Cooper recalls. "He never related what his counterparts said. Therefore people would tell him a lot, confident there wouldn't be any splashy results—any one-day news." It was not known for almost ten years that Cooper personally was able to convince Eisenhower and Dulles that Nehru's neutralism was sincere and not just a maneuver.

Cooper says he thought it was a mistake for Nehru to make Kashmir part of India; yet he says he told Nehru he could understand why India would feel this need out of concern for securing its borders against China. Too, Cooper was sympathetic with Nehru's deep concern that the Eisenhower administration was supporting the military buildup of India's neighbor, Pakistan. In 1961 Professor Galbraith, after conferring with "wise without pretense" Cooper, wrote, "He [Cooper] told me with some reluctance that he had made it clear to Nehru when he was ambassador that his position on the Pakistan arms buildup was not the same as that of Dulles and that he was urging a change."

Also, Cooper was pressing the administration in Washington to ask Congress to switch foreign aid from a year-to-year basis to a longer period allowing recipient countries to plan their development more efficiently. Once again it would bring Cooper up against conservative colleagues who were grumbling about "ungrateful India" and "backdoor financing." In response Cooper compared United States and Russian aid programs. As he said in the Senate five years later, still pursuing the same aim of longer range and hence more efficient foreign aid, "I do not say that the Russian program is superior to ours in all respects. Many of our Point Four programs are humane and go to basic needs.

"But, at present, the Soviet Union's program is superior to ours in the respect that it provides long-term loans . . . at low interest rates. For this reason the countries take the aid of the Soviet Union because the aid is available at once for their industrial development."

Cooper was finding it incomprehensible that American administrations, aware of the many years required to develop and create new industries and of the needs for capital, should be so shortsighted as to expect underdeveloped nations to plan and build on a one-year basis. He was also noting that, unlike the nations of Europe with which he was so familiar, a country of impoverished people such as India with its annual per capita income of $90 had no alternative to governmental development—that is, to economic socialism—as its formula for industrial growth.

Beginning within two months of his and Mrs. Cooper's arrival, the ambassador wrote himself and delivered to Indian audiences a series of speeches that were "pure Cooper" in their delineation of what he perceived to be American motivations and shared Indo-American democratic values. To an audience of Indians who had studied or worked in the United States and Americans doing the same in India, Cooper began a speech in April 1955 much as he might have at a family reunion in Pulaski County or a class gathering at Centre College.

"It has always seemed to me that the association of students in schools and colleges is one of the happiest of all the experiences of life," he said. "We find there that we know relatively very little; and out of this realization grow humility and tolerance toward others.

"In its very nature, the spirit of inquiry must be for truth; and truth applies to all people. Animating all is the idealism of young men and women who have faith that their search for truth may better the world and the lot of mankind."

In that optimistic vein, Cooper summoned his listeners to examine the commonality of Indian and United States aspirations. "The underlying goal of American foreign policy is to make it possible for our people to live in peace and to enjoy the blessings and fruits of individual liberty. It is our hope also that freedom will advance in the world. We hold steadfastly to the objective of a peaceful world where nations will settle their differences through negotiation—the vision from which the United Nations was born."

Yet it was not cloying naivete that Cooper purveyed. He recognized that although some might have considered U.S. disarmament unrealistic and foolhardy after World War II, it had in fact been an inevitable outgrowth of American popular desire that peace be "given its chance to prevail." In another speech that year in Madras, home of India's fiery and often anti-U.S. Krishna Menon, Cooper cited Machiavelli, Hegel, and Grotius in acknowledging that no nation's foreign policy always is based entirely on moral right.

"There is a realm between the ethical bases and the high purposes of a nation—the realm of means or practice—where interest, experience, and even expediency play their part in the development of policy," he conceded to his Indian listeners.

76

He was stressing for all free nations, he said, the imperative of "a kind of ethical minimum" necessary for securing a peaceful and unified world order.

It could be found, Cooper said, in U.S. recognition that "while democracy is not a fixed system and that its form differs in various lands . . . its ethical roots are the same: belief in individual worth, in his capacity for development, in his capability to think and act with reason, and to improve peacefully his political and social conditions." Cooper said he had found this reflected in the concept in ancient Hindu law called *Dharma*—that one must do the "right" thing simply because it is the right thing.

Later visitors to India such as Senator Stuart Symington said it was no wonder Nehru was found "always quoting the ambassador from Kentucky," as Symington put it. Nehru frequently applauded what he called Cooper's "always candid statements of his government's position."

"Nehru combined idealism and paternalism," Lorraine Cooper said in 1974. "His own newspaper had asked, 'Will Nehru be a dictator?' but he *chose* the parliamentary system. He was a poor organizer but he was extremely close to the people. They spoke of *darshan*—an emanation from someone good. Why did two or three hundred thousand people assemble time and again to see and hear him? *Darshan*—a superior being."

As for the prime minister's daughter and eventual successor, Indira Gandhi, Mrs. Cooper said, "I admire her inordinately. She is a brilliant politician with a toughness her father didn't have—but less elevating."

Mrs. Cooper made the comment long before the 1975 political crisis that led Indira Gandhi to order the arrest of political opponents and impose severe limits upon the domestic and foreign press. Of course, neither of the Coopers could have anticipated this twenty years earlier. Yet there was a certain prescience in parts of Ambassador Cooper's speech in New Delhi in April 1955.

"It is wholly for the good of mankind that 800 millions

of [Asian] people have become independent. They are facing their new problems with faith and decisive action but they are nevertheless very difficult problems. . . . Some so-called revolutions have represented only a change in domination, and it is an unhappy page of history that many true revolutions growing from the people and giving hope for a time were crushed by new assertions of power. . . . The democratic system is a difficult one. It is sometimes slow because it asks a large assumption of cooperation and responsibility upon the part of its people, as well as on the part of their leaders. . . ."

Within three months after the Coopers' arrival in New Delhi, the word drifting back to Washington was that they had taken India's government community "by storm." One helpful element was that the ambassador, while not abandoning his totally unmethodical approach to administrative detail, was unexpectedly keeping appointments on time (much to the confusion of Mrs. Cooper who had based her planning on the assumption that "while I am a clock, John is a calendar").

News reached Kentucky of the Coopers' ingenious successes in hospitality. There was talk of how Mrs. Cooper often conversed in Russian with the Soviet ambassador to India, Mikhail Menshikov; the president of an Indian university, upon finding himself served at the Coopers' with a main dinner course labeled "Roast Schmoo," exclaimed to Cooper, "Excellency, I see you, too, are a devotee of Mr. Al Capp."

One Kentuckian visiting India in 1955 wrote home in detail. She described how Mrs. Cooper had transformed the appearance of the ambassadorial residence, which had looked, she said, like a Grand Rapids showroom. "There now are dead white walls, yards and yards of beautifully cool white chintz printed with just-right blue roses in the drawing room and dark blue and light blue Indian fabrics in the library, with accents of red in both. The effect is cool beyond belief." In the residence yard

Lorraine Cooper had planted Bibb lettuce, that delicacy originally developed in Kentucky's capital city of Frankfort. The visitor from Kentucky, to illustrate her impression that Lorraine Cooper was putting "her whole soul into every party," described an affair at which Nehru and Krishna Menon were the honored guests:

". . . The most beautiful and successful party I've ever seen in my life," she wrote. "The 24 guests seated at three round tables were treated to good, light music drifting in from a pianist playing in the library. After dinner, there was lighting out on the terrace by dozens of candles and cool, blue lights in the trees around the edge of the garden. The French ambassador kept wandering around saying under his breath, 'Mon dieu! Quelle beauté!' "

Concluded the Kentucky observer: "She is doing a grand and wonderful job and John seems as happy as a clam at high tide. I think she is just what he needed and it proves that he is as smart as I think he is, that he could recognize it."

Domestic U.S. politics and Cooper's abiding hunger for the Senate intervened after April 30, 1956. That was the day Senator Alben Barkley fell dead while making a speech at Washington and Lee University. "Right away, the pressure was on John," says Thruston Morton. The GOP thought it had a chance to get control of the U.S. Senate. In Kentucky, Morton would be trying for the seat held by Democrat Earle C. Clements. A Cooper run against former Governor Lawrence Wetherby for the four years of the unexpired Barkley term might be a potent political mix.

Cooper remembers his feelings in New Delhi: "India is too important." His brother Dick affirms, "John really didn't want to run." Appeals to Cooper came from Morton; from George Norton, Morton's brother-in-law and Cooper's Yale classmate; and finally, from presidential aide Sherman Adams. There were also earthier, made-in-Kentucky appeals. Cooper received in New

79

Delhi a transworld telephone call from T. C. Sizemore, Republican chairman of rural Owsley County: "John, get back here and run against Wetherby," Sizemore exclaimed. "To hell with old Nero!"

"I have to know the President wants me to run," said John Sherman Cooper. When Dwight Eisenhower made the request personally, Cooper acquiesced.

In India the word of the Coopers' departure was treated as bad news. Said the *Times* of India, "He had something of the old world charm of Kentucky, with a genteel reticence and reserve not always associated with the new world. In Mrs. Cooper he possessed a gracious and highly intelligent helpmate with a political perceptiveness that was acute and agile."

Before embarking upon the campaign for the Barkley seat, John and Lorraine Cooper took a vacation back in Somerset where Mrs. Cooper had visited only once. That was before their marriage which had set some Pulaski County people to wondering what John was doing getting hitched up to that fancy, rich divorcée woman.

Generally, Kentuckians proved as hospitable to Mrs. Cooper as her husband's kin. "It had already become my adopted state but I've been eternally surprised at how helpful and courteous people were to me from the very beginning," Mrs. Cooper says.

But there was some evidence that she had to work at it a bit. According to columnist Drew Pearson, awed fascination was the reaction of 93-year-old Somersetian Ben V. Smith, Jr., when he first saw Lorraine Cooper with her parasol: "That wife of John Cooper's was walking around the Courthouse Square with a white umbrella and it wasn't even rainin'!"

The Pearson report (citing Smith's age as 103) gave the campaign a bizarre start. Smith, who died a week or two later, had been for almost a half century the county Democratic chairman. His son wrote an angry letter to the *Louisville Courier-Journal* which had carried the

Pearson column, denying that his father had made the statement. The women in Somerset were used to carrying parasols, he said; his father and the ambassador's father, though of different political parties, had been lifelong friends—and he and all the other Smiths intended to vote for Cooper for senator.

Looking back on the period from the perspective of 1974, Vermont Senator George D. Aiken wrote, "During the period . . . when he was ambassador to India, I feel that John Cooper's low-key and humane approach to the problems of people did much to keep our relations with that country on a more workable plane. Not all of our diplomats have a non-inflammatory way of dealing with officials of foreign countries and, in some instances, the United States has paid a rather high price for their lack of tact and consideration."

Perhaps not even India's Nehru sensed in 1956 that ahead lay the apogee of Cooper's influence upon U.S. foreign affairs relating to India as well as to a menaced free Berlin and a bisected Germany, to international arms control, and most of all to Southeast Asia. For with the clear election victory he won in November 1956 Cooper was on his way to sixteen influential years in the United States Senate, to include two full terms of his own and a place on the Foreign Relations Committee previously denied him by his in-and-out record.

Events destined to affect Cooper through the rest of his career marked that 1956 election season. Hungarians revolted against Soviet domination. Israel, Britain, and France moved to take over the Suez Canal. And in one of the elections that kept the GOP from senate control, Idaho elected a 32-year-old Democratic lawyer named Frank Church to replace veteran conservative Republican Senator Herman Welker.

The chubby-faced Church was as much the orator as Cooper was the mumbler. Church was then more internationally hawkish than Cooper. If Cooper would be likened to a deep, quiet country river, Church was a bouncy western mountain stream. But thirteen years later the old "C" and the young "C" were to become an odd couple historically linked—one as spokesman, the other as backstage tactician—in the effort to edge Congress back into its traditional role in foreign policy and warmaking.

7

HERITAGE, experience, and his approach to human relations shaped John Sherman Cooper for a key foreign affairs role during the nation's harrowing decade and a half between 1956 and 1972.

The period needed someone in the United States Senate bound in support of the country's military strength but grittily dedicated to espousing the use of negotiations whenever risk allowed it. The period needed someone to stand up to presidents and foreign adversaries while continuing to retain their respect and trust. There was a demand for a man hanging tough on constitutional principles even while many constituents and political colleagues would temporarily leave him lonely in his stance.

John Sherman Cooper filled that bill.

President John F. Kennedy sent him on a critical, secret mission to Moscow, rightly confident that Soviet leaders might show Cooper the candor necessary to allow a realistic assessment of Russia's aggressive intentions. Presidents Lyndon Johnson and Richard Nixon also leaned upon Cooper, even though he became the rallying point in the Senate against the spread and escalation of hostilities in Southeast Asia. Johnson sent him back to the UN, where Cooper stood up to the Russians without baiting them. He also made Cooper in 1964 a member of the Warren Commission to investigate the assassination of President Kennedy. Nixon sought Cooper's counsel in the events that led to the first SALT talks that in 1972 saw the permanent curbing of Soviet-U.S. defensive weapons. The background for this was Cooper's senate leadership of a three-year battle against U.S. deployment of an antiballistic missile system he had concluded was untested and unwise. The battle's specific objectives were never won, but the broader impacts were profound.

In 1971, partly under the spur of the *New York Times* publication of classified military documents on American involvement in Vietnam—the Pentagon Papers—Cooper anticipated later history by introducing a bill that called upon the CIA to keep Congress more adequately informed of intelligence involving spying and national security.

Through all of this, Cooper escaped rancor from those with whom he differed.

When he needed confidential information on Soviet disappointments with such a system to bolster his efforts against the ABM, the CIA supplied it.

As Cooper became one of the most persistent critics of Vietnam bombing in the Johnson administration, Lyndon and Ladybird Johnson nevertheless remained on friendly terms with the Coopers (as they did not with more strident critics) and Lorraine Cooper counts Mrs. Johnson "one of the best president's wives there could ever be."

And when, beginning in 1969, Cooper teamed up with Idaho's Democratic Senator Frank Church on the series of amendments limiting the Vietnam War, known as Cooper-Church, Secretary of State Henry Kissinger slyly let it be known where his preferences lay. As Cooper smilingly recalls, it was an occasion when Church had publicly berated Kissinger and reporters asked the secretary if this denoted a feud. "Why, no, Senator Church and I are good friends," Kissinger replied. "He calls me Henry—and I call him Cooper."

In tracing Cooper's influence through the 1956–1972

span, it is intriguing to explore even further the chemistry of how he managed.

The unmistakable influence of having been steeped in the traditions and mores of Kentucky, a place where (along with a distinct strain of violence) compromise was part of the fabric since before the Civil War—that is the analysis of Cooper's conduct in these critical years offered by Barry Bingham, Sr., who was editor and publisher of the Louisville daily newspapers during the heights of Cooper's career.

"John has always been a marvelous man for getting along with both sides, not in any posed false way but sincerely," says Bingham, who genially recalls the ribbing suggestion of one former staffer that Cooper was "invented" by the Bingham papers so they would have one Republican they could editorially admire. (Indeed, Bingham maintains that had Cooper only been born fifty miles further west, he would have been a Democrat.)

"He has been a fine combination of the down-to-earth quality of Kentucky's mountain counties and the finesse and *politesse* of the Bluegrass section," Bingham says. "He truly combines the best of both sections, in my view. Although he can be canny, he does not have that suspiciousness and that put-off way of playing hands close to the vest that are also mountain characteristics.

"The result is that when you sit down with him, you say, 'This man really trusts me and I wouldn't lie to him.'"

Lorraine Cooper, too, found this quality in her husband. "You might call his care in making judgments 'suspicious' but it isn't really that," she says. "It's something I've seen also in Tommy [career diplomat Llewellyn] Thompson: it is a way of looking at all sides of a situation that to me had appeared to be just one-sided. Add to that John's antenna about people—even while he is looking so nice and innocent—and the result is . . . well, it sounds vainglorious coming from me but the result is that John has never been an amateur!"

Senate aide William Miller, who says he "found decency" when he left the State Department to join Cooper in 1967, puts it this way: "When I'd betray astonishment at how wise and sophisticated he was, complete with moments when he'd quote from Shakespeare, the Bible, or one of the poets, he'd wave it off by telling me he was a country fellow who'd merely tried to learn his lessons well."

When it came to the CIA supplying information to Cooper that in some cases would reveal the agency's flaws, Miller says, "partly it was because they knew he wouldn't leak it or misuse it. But also it was his way of not giving the impression he knew as much as he did. That was his method of gauging character and gaining information."

Miller cites an occasion when a man came from the State Department's India desk to consult Senator Cooper about a rupee-dollar exchange question. "The man patronized the Senator all over the place—until the Senator suddenly dropped a key figure and a key name and the man knew he'd made a fool of himself."

If one regrettable aberration were chosen in the sixteen years that saw the zenith of the Cooper career, it would be the Gulf of Tonkin resolution, voted in August 1964 at the behest of President Johnson and Defense Secretary Robert McNamara. The resolution laid the groundwork of presidential authority for involvement of vast numbers of American troops in Southeast Asia without prior congressional approval. "The presidency rampant," historian Arthur M. Schlesinger, Jr., called it.

Under the duress of North Vietnamese attacks upon U.S. destroyers in the Gulf of Tonkin in that summer of 1964, only two senators (Wayne Morse of Oregon and Ernest Gruening of Alaska) voted against the resolution, which proved to be a blank check for presidential step-ups of troop involvements in Asia under the mantle of "preventing aggression." Of later suggestions that the destroyer attacks may have been deliberately provoked to create an "incident" for congressional attention, Cooper says no such doubts were raised at the time and no proof has ever been found.

But Cooper was one of a handful who questioned the resolution on the floor, even while later voting "aye" out of a reluctance to disrupt presidential handling of the destroyer incident. As Schlesinger notes, it was Cooper who asked Senator Fulbright, floor manager for the resolution, whether "if the President decided it was necessary to use such force as could lead into war, we will give that authority by this resolution?"

Fulbright answered, "That is the way I would interpret it." He added, with an optimism he came bitterly to regret, "I have no doubt that the President will consult with Congress in case a major change in present policy becomes necessary."

Cooper was first among the few quoted by the *New York Times* that day as feeling "a vague uneasiness" about the new authority to be voted to the president. "There is a difference between protecting our own forces and taking action which would lead to a third world war," Cooper said. He continued, "Perhaps events are inevitable," but he hoped the president "would use the pause [then in effect in Vietnam] and would take advantage of every possibility afforded by the Geneva accords of 1954 and the machinery of the United Nations to get an agreement before we find ourselves moving progressively forward to a third world war."

In the next two years Cooper was one of the few in the Senate who drove hardest to persuade President Johnson to halt the bombing of North Vietnam.

The following year, while Johnson was insisting that it was by Hanoi's choice that the war continued and Cooper was disagreeing and saying that first steps toward peace should and could be America's, Cooper still called Johnson "a man of good intentions who wants peace," and he recognized that the cessation of bombing was a difficult decision for the president.

It is a reflection of the strange ways of the Senate—and of the national press—that not until ten years after his 1957 return to the Senate was Cooper given a place on the Foreign Relations Committee and proper national media attention to his Vietnam role, which dated back to 1954 when Cooper joined Senator Mansfield to say on BBC, after the French surrender at Dien Bien Phu, that the U.S. should never consider armed forces help as long as there was any opening for negotiation. "Maybe that long wait for the Foreign Relations Committee went into his character, deepened his patience," muses Lawrence Forgy, now a Louisville attorney, who as a youth was a Cooper campaign chauffeur and looked after the senator's "Don't Rain On My Parade" martini bag.

Cooper was on the committee five months before, as the *New York Times* reported, "the gentle, white-haired former Ambassador to India provided a suitable figure for [President Johnson's foreign policy] Senate critics to rally around." In what was termed a major speech, Cooper urged the administration—"in full confidence that rises from strength"—to limit Southeast Asia bombing, "if bomb we must," to infiltration routes into South Vietnam. Such a step, he said, could serve as a new peace initiative, and any risks to American troops on the scene would be far less than the risks of an expanded war involving China or Russia. He digressed from his prepared text for a typical Cooper other-point-of-view suggestion: China's Chou En-lai might well be viewing America's military presence in the area in the same threatening light that the United States had justifiably seen Russia with its missiles in Cuba in 1962.

Among those who congratulated Cooper on his speech were Democrats Church, Wayne Morse, and Mike Mansfield and Republicans George Aiken of Vermont and Thruston Morton of Kentucky. Cooper now stresses that Aiken and Mansfield were as important as Church and he were in the long effort to get the Vietnam hostilities wound down. He also found himself "tickled" by the

Kentucky-New York axis he often formed with Senator Jacob Javits, whom he admires as "a human being with a keen intelligence."

The pulling power that the press noted in Cooper in 1967 had for years been known to his senate colleagues. Among these was John F. Kennedy. In December 1960, it was a newly elected but not yet inaugurated President Kennedy who chose Cooper for the mission until recently kept secret, a fact-finding trip to New Delhi and Moscow. The objective was to obtain a realistic assessment of Soviet government attitudes to guide the new administration.

"I went with a long list of questions from John Kennedy," Cooper recalls. "Mrs. Cooper and I reached Moscow the day after the closing of the international Communist Party meeting that marked the beginning of the Sino-Soviet breach." Tommy Thompson—"one of our very best," Cooper says—was there as U.S. ambassador to Moscow to help in Cooper's task.

"Khruschev didn't even go to see the Chinese off at the airport; instead he went off mad to his *dacha* so I missed him," Cooper says. "But among those with whom I did confer were Kuznetzov, Gromyko—and Mikoyan, who survived Stalin and 'em all in the top structure." (Cooper notes also Gromyko's survival factor but says he never operated at Mikoyan's level.)

In addition to Russian estrangement from the Chinese, another development seemed to lend encouragement to the value of the conversations with the Soviet leaders. A major international group of scientists had just met in Moscow. "Walt Rostow had sent back a glowing report," Cooper remembers. "But he and the others had only seen the scientists," Mrs. Cooper adds.

All was pleasantness when the Coopers joined the scientist group for a party at the Thompsons' ambassadorial residence. But Thompson was "grateful" when Cooper turned down interview requests from American television network reporters, eschewing what Mrs.

Cooper says is "an unfortunate tendency for a politician abroad to say anything he wants to, leaving the State Department and the Administration to take the blame."

The reason for special gratitude for diplomatic silence in this instance was that Cooper went to his meetings with the Soviet leaders fresh from a study of the latest communist party communique which he recalls had blasted the United States vitriolically as a world enemy and imperialist aggressor—"all such talk like that," Cooper says drily.

"I said to Mikoyan, 'You have called the United States an aggressor. Do you mean it? You know it is not true.'"

Cooper continues: "Mikoyan's answer was 'no, no, that was all dialectics'—and in the same breath—'we speak objectively and that is our conclusion.' All he seemed to want to talk was trade, trade, trade. But then he said he could see no difference in the recent U.S. election between Kennedy and Nixon so far as their policy statements were concerned; they both showed enmity toward the Soviet Union."

From this and other talks Cooper says he found "a chilling situation—not just frightening but chilling." Mrs. Cooper adds, "The Russian government officials John saw all were tough as a boot."

Says Cooper with grim recollection, "The report I wrote for John Kennedy was very pessimistic. I predicted a very rough time. Later, after Kennedy as president had met with Khruschev in Austria, he told me, 'John, I wish I'd paid more attention. You were so right!'"

The relationship with John Kennedy had grown from service together on the Senate Labor Committee and a social friendship, as well as a natural affinity transcending differences of party. From Cooper's return to the Senate onward, the Kennedys and the Coopers were dinner guests at each others' homes (although when the Coopers so entertained them after Kennedy's 1960 election as president, the Pulaski County GOP chairman went to the Cooper kin in Somerset asking angrily, "What's John mean havin' those people to supper?").

In 1958 and again the next year, both men combined to lead the Congress into backing U.S. and international agencies in commitments of help to India's and Pakistan's development efforts; Cooper still believes they helped keep India a force for peace and democratic values throughout the next fifteen years.

While certainly not on the same cordial footing as with Kennedy, Cooper found positive values in then-Vice President Nixon, and (despite a family preference for Nelson Rockefeller) he did not shirk party duty in behalf of Nixon's 1960 race against Kennedy. Indeed, it was under Cooper's adroit questioning that Nixon manifested his early commitment to the principle of superpower negotiation, when the pair appeared together on regional television from Louisville in 1959. Cooper says he knew that even then Nixon was looking for an "opening" in international stalemate and believes the 1959 discussion was a striking index of this.

Nixon had just returned from his visit to Moscow, highlighted by his headline-making confrontation with Khruschev in front of a refrigerator at the Moscow international trade fair. Khruschev's visit to the United States was imminent.

Cooper: "I notice one of the first things you said to him—in that confrontation—was that his country could not deliver threats, ultimatums to the United States or to the democratic countries."

Nixon: "The time has come, I told him, when it doesn't make any difference whether one nation or the other at a particular time has got a better missile or a bigger bomb. . . . No nation, no matter how strong it is, no matter what temporary advantage it has in any one field, can develop the power today to knock out the other major power. . . ."

Cooper: "You know, of course, that there is concern in this country, among many people who remember the

91

atrocities and the evil tyranny of Russia and Mr. Khruschev, about his coming here. And also many believe it
will discourage the people in the eastern European nations. But I gather from what you say that . . . you
believe this opportunity to see overrides these considera-
tions."

Nixon: ". . . It isn't that I expect [Khruschev's]
coming here is going to convert him to our system of
government. It isn't because I think his coming here is
going to settle the problems of the world, either . . . it is
because there is no alternative, it appears to me, to
talking—to having him sit down across the table from the
President of the United States. . . ."

Then Cooper, with words about the importance of the
United States keeping itself secure, asked Nixon to reit-
erate his discovery that he had found immense desire for
peace among the ordinary people of Poland and Russia.
"In the rural communities we found perhaps the greatest
friendship of all in the Soviet Union," Nixon recalled.

"I think that's always true," said Cooper.

Nixon: "Of course you're a little prejudiced, John."

Cooper: "Yes, I'm a little prejudiced, because I come
from a rural community and also from the mountain part
of my state. Well, in closing, I do think you would say that
if we are ever going to have peace or make any solutions,
we do have to keep these exchanges and keep talking.
Isn't that true?"

Nixon: "Absolutely. This is the only hope for the future, unless we want to end up in a war that will destroy us
all."

Cooper remained consistent for negotiation, through
the Soviet Union's building of the Berlin wall, the U.S.
confrontation with the Soviets over missiles in Castro's
Cuba, the 1967 outbreak of hostilities in the Middle East
and the threats to European security occasioned under
Charles DeGaulle when he withdrew French forces from
NATO.

In the teeth of Khruschev ultimatums in 1961 to close

access to West Berlin, Cooper won some colleagues' plaudits by backing a "stand firm" policy but warning ". . . if the phrase 'stand firm' means the fixed position that the President ought not examine the realities of the situation, or communicate with Soviet Russia, or take any honorable means to prevent the commencement of hostilities which might expand into a third world war, I disagree. And I disagree unequivocally with those who, using the term 'stand firm,' consider it appeasement if any attempt is made by members of Congress or by the President to discuss Berlin except in dogmatic or belligerent terms."

As Cooper said in a 1975 letter, what came first for him—"my basic principle"—was the security of the nation. With that came a regard for the constitutional authority of the president "to act on his own initiative to defend our territory, armed forces, and people when attacked." But after deferring to the needs of sheer national survival and proper presidential flexibility, then—often under the most stressful circumstances—Cooper turned his voice and his influence against rash, partisan talk and against usurpation of Congress' authority to make the decisions about involving the nation in war.

In March 1962 after the Soviet Union had resumed atmospheric nuclear testing and it was reported President Kennedy would do the same, Cooper supported the president. But he added, "We should continue our efforts to reach a true and enforceable agreement with the Soviet Union."

"It is argued by some that negotiations are futile, and there is much in the record to support this view. But our free system of government is based on concepts different from those of the Soviet Union—on ethical and religious principles. Even though we may resume atomic tests, and under the circumstances I believe it necessary, we owe it to the people of the world and our principles to continue our efforts to reach agreement with the Soviet Union."

Later that year, during the Cuban missile crisis which

Cooper called "one of the most dangerous events since World War II," he again supported a resolution endorsing the use of presidential powers even through the stage of a blockade—but again Cooper admonished, ". . . I do not believe that the Cuban situation is one to be used as a political gambit. It is too dangerous to the security of our country to be either political or reckless in what we say or do."

As the decade moved on, the same blend of perceptions marked his personal reinvolvement with the stability of NATO, for whose meetings he annually took time away from the Senate. Following the 1967 meeting, he wrote a detailed memorandum that delineated the importance of continued NATO troop strengths in Europe as a force for peace. "It would be extremely foolish," wrote Cooper, "to assert that the Soviet Union of 1967 is the Soviet Union of 1949. There have been important changes. Perhaps internal politics and economic developments have made the Soviets more conservative, in the sense they may be less inclined to run large risks. Kosygin and Brezhnev are not Khruschev and Khruschev is not Stalin . . . but the capabilities of the Soviet Union do not give grounds for complacency. . . ."

Harlan Cleveland, then permanent U.S. representative to the North Atlantic Council, called this in a letter to Cooper, "one of the clearest outlines of NATO's present and future that I've had the pleasure of reading." A measure of the level at which Cooper was doing special duty came later that year when, following attendance at a NATO meeting in Europe, Cooper wrote to British Foreign Secretary George Brown, "On my return to Washington I delivered your message to the President [Johnson], and to him alone."

The stubborn strength behind his diffident, halting manner was also revealed in 1968 when with Senator Stuart Symington he returned as a delegate to the UN General Assembly for a session of the UN Legal Committee concerned with a definition of "aggression." That

August, just three months earlier, Russian and other Warsaw Pact troops had occupied Czechoslovakia, ending that nation's brief bid for a more liberal version of communism.

Cooper struck out at the Soviet action. He recalled that it had been at Soviet insistence that the General Assembly, despite reservations, had established a special committee to draft a definition of "aggression." Now the Soviets had marched in and thrown down a neighboring government.

Three facts were "cardinal," Cooper said.

"So far as relations between the U.S.S.R. and Czechoslovakia are concerned, aggression had already been defined by treaty . . . indeed, for over three decades," and internal "disturbances or counterrevolutions" had specifically been banned as an excuse for moving in troops.

"The Soviet invasion and occupation were so clear a violation of the existing law of aggression, laid down by the UN charter, that the Soviet Union itself abandoned its early pretenses of explaining or justifying this action in any terms consistent with the charter.

"Far from seeking to justify its action under the charter, the Soviet Union has subsequently devised and announced to the world a new doctrine unknown in international law. . . ."

For weeks, Cooper noted, the Russians had tried in vain to produce "even one Czechoslovak citizen whom it could present as speaking for the government of Czechoslovakia—or even on his own behalf—as having invited the occupying forces." In fact, Cooper said, the Soviet Union now was claiming the right to intervene by force against independent countries whenever the "class struggle" seemed to require it—and this doctrine had to be counted "a monstrous regression."

Cooper reminisced in a 1974 interview, "Oh, that fella [the Soviet representative] got so mad! Jacob Malik, the Soviet delegation leader, protested to our mission about my statement." Yet, Cooper said, "I had tried to be correct and not inflammatory—that was my aim." Symington, on the scene, recalls the universal respect with which Cooper was greeted upon his return to the UN. The Kentuckian himself, looking back with that country-itch for examining another person's motivations, reflects that at the time the Russians were being dogged by their widened rift with China and had suffered the setback of being told to withdraw their troops from Egypt. Even bullies are meaner when they feel bruised and threatened, Cooper reckoned.

It was Cooper's 1967 move to the Senate Foreign Relations Committee that led him to take on 35-year-old William Miller as special aide.

"He liked the enthusiasm and perspective of the young, he got solace from anyone hopeful . . . ," says Miller, in 1975 the staff chief for the senate CIA investigating committee under Senator Church.

"Of American foreign policy, Senator Cooper felt that it had slipped into a void. He thought our world purposes had become tarnished and demeaned—in terms of our generous national nature, a terrible loss. That's why he so valued strategic arms control and more perceptive and long-range foreign aid."

Miller is a Williams College and Oxford product, a former instructor in Elizabethan literature at Harvard who had gone to work in the Foreign Service and for the State Department and become disenchanted. He met Cooper first in India in 1966 while an assistant to Secretary of State Dean Rusk, with whom Cooper was traveling as President Johnson's representative at the funeral of Prime Minister Shastri. They met again in Saigon. Soon thereafter, when Miller was considering a return to college teaching, Cooper telephoned him.

"I need help on the Foreign Relations Committee," the senator said. "It'll help me enormously—and it may even help you." Miller says, "For me, it proved to be a liberation after the State Department, where so much had been a lie and a deceit."

On the wall of Miller's new senate cubbyhole office there soon hung a sign reading, "ABM is an Edsel." In 1967, through what some capital reporters suddenly discovered was Cooper's judicial eye for evidence, the senator had spotted serious flaws in Pentagon arguments for an ABM defense system. "If the research man from the Pentagon was shaky about it, Defense Secretary McNamara was all the more so, he was all over the lot in his statements," Cooper said. And Cooper saw the ABM as a spur to intensified Soviet-U.S. nuclear rivalry.

One day in April 1968 when Cooper was reading a Miller memo on the subject and Miller spotted him going through the throat-clearing habit that was a sign of Cooper appreciation, the aide knew ABM action was imminent. Cooper moved to delay Senate authorization of an ABM program until the Pentagon could report more thoroughly on research and specific costs. Defeat by only three votes showed Cooper that many other senators were similarly uncertain; it also won him an important ally in Michigan's Democratic Senator Philip A. Hart, who said much later, "Cooper is regarded as someone who just goes where the facts lead. Party labels don't disturb him. Personalities are not involved. Sincerity is never questioned. When you put all that together, you've got a guy who can move."

Says Miller, "To begin with, Senator Cooper knew certain things about ABM. He knew there would be catastrophe if the missile race went unstopped, but he knew no particulars. But once he made up his mind—saw a chance in the Senate even for an imperfect test vote—there was no stopping him.

"Over four years he conducted a running seminar with physicists, arms makers, strategists. He studied and studied." Sometimes, to do his thinking, he made "marvelous escapes," like the occasion when Miller found him on his back behind a wall outside the Senate Office Building, looking at the sky.

"Yet I found his pace was just right for the Senate. He

97

never used parliamentary tricks, never cut off debate or tried to time a vote. He simply knew every member well and had his respect, he was a great vote counter, and his sense of timing was unerring."

As for Cooper's Kentucky constituents who in many cases were puzzled by his position on ABM, the senator says, "I always explained why I was doing a thing. I usually had facts upon which to base my position. When they knew more, they would tell me." He proved the efficacy of this approach by addressing the American Legion on the ABM and winning it over. The group, strongly in favor of ABM, gave him a rousing hand.

In the end, although Cooper and Hart never won a senate vote on ABM, unprecedented opening of the defense budget to senate scrutiny produced warranted appropriations cuts amounting to several billion dollars. The effect of these publicized cuts in hastening the first SALT talks with the Russians had already been anticipated by Cooper the day after Richard Nixon's first inauguration; he went to the White House to encourage the president's taking up a quick, favorable Moscow response to an "era of negotiations" theme in the inaugural address.

Along with ABM, domestic issues brought Cooper into differences with his new president. Miller says the senator "agonized" when it came to a decision in the Nixon nominations of G. Harold Carswell and Clement Haynesworth for the Supreme Court. In the latter case, Cooper's vote was one of those most impatiently awaited and watched, and a factor in his "nay" was a long distance call from his 90-year-old mother. "John," she said, "Judge Haynesworth isn't the man." That was the remarkable lady who the family remembers was wont to field questions about her son with the snappy comment "Which son? I have three" (to which the senator's brother Dick adds with a wry grin, "Yes—John, John, and John").

Cooper recalls that following his mother's telephone

call about Haynesworth, a colleague to whom Cooper mentioned it tipped *Newsweek* magazine which ran the episode under the heading, "A Special Kind of Lobbying." As a result, Cooper received hundreds of telegrams saying "Obey your mother."

No such whimsy accompanied his "yes" vote on President Nixon's equally unsuccessful Carswell court nomination, a vote which Cooper admits he does not now consider to have been "a great judgment."

He explains, "I did believe that he [Carswell] was being improperly treated by some members of the Judiciary Committee and particularly by the New York Bar Association whose president at the time had been a classmate of mine at Harvard Law School. He charged first that Carswell's record on civil rights was bad, but gave up on that when two distinguished lawyers testified that they had checked his record and it was good.

"Then, in a meeting in my senate office, they began to criticize his record. I think I have some feeling that I rationalized [all this]—I knew he had no outstanding record as a federal judge—and that my vote was a rationalization."

Cooper's vote against the Haynesworth nomination was most strongly influenced by two lower-court cases in which Cooper felt special financial interest should have led Haynesworth to have disqualified himself. The vote brought the senator one of those home front diatribes:

"Haynesworth was dumped not because of qualifications," said the *Times-Journal* of Russell Springs, Kentucky, in a county bordering Pulaski County, "but rather because he holds some views not unlike a majority of people in this area and throughout the South. . . . His rejection is indicative of vast power still held by the North Eastern Mafia like the Kennedys, the Javitses and Brooks, and of the Southerner, John Sherman Cooper, who doesn't seem to think like we do today, but more like the rich widow he married. Though he is from adjoining

Pulaski County, we should let him understand . . . that if he intends to represent Kentucky as a Senator, or Governor, he should think and act like a Kentuckian."

But this outburst did not match in intensity or magnitude the protests sent Cooper's way as he pursued from 1969 on the series of amendments aimed at curbing further U.S. military involvement in Southeast Asia. The amendments became the first moves since Korea and the Gulf of Tonkin toward redressing congressional loss of authority in warmaking decisions. In 1970, writing to a Kentucky supporter who had the wistful notion that the 69-year-old senator might run for governor if only the Cooper-Church amendments could be forgotten, Cooper said with remarkable understatement, "I have had a pretty hard time with letters from Kentucky about this amendment."

Yet he felt secure in his position on the war, which took two forms that appeared contradictory. He frequently balked at senate actions he thought would tie the hands of the president in protecting Americans in Southeast Asia. But he was resolute in curbing presidential moves to broaden the fighting.

Looking back on the period three years later, Cooper said, "The Cooper-Church amendments did not usurp the constitutional authority of the President. They were based on the *one certain constitutional* authority of the Congress to bring a war to an end, or prevent its expansion (as one of our amendments was directed to prevent the Vietnam War from expanding into Cambodia and Laos): that is, to deny funds except to protect our forces as they withdrew."

It was reminiscent of the way the power of the purse was seen by Thomas Jefferson, who said the best check on war was to put the power of initiating it with those who appropriate the money rather than with those who spend it.

Washington observers now see the teaming of Republican Cooper and Idaho's Democratic Church as having been an ideal double-edged sword for cutting the way in behalf of diminishing the war.

Unlike such more-precipitous congressional doves as Senators George McGovern and Mark Hatfield of Oregon or Charles Goodell of New York, Cooper and Church respected the need for leaving President Nixon sufficient flexibility to protect American soldiers already in Southeast Asia while inhibiting use of this as a stratagem. In the spectrum of dovishness, they occupied centrist perches, which enhanced their odds of collecting enough votes to temper war's escalation. Cooper had the experience, and his enduring Kentucky earnestness and thoroughness still held the ear of the White House and of swing-vote colleagues. As Church admiringly said of Cooper's quiet workings in 1970, "The most effective militance is that which perseveres for principle."

Church had not only the intellect but the articulateness. As a youth in 1941, he had been the national winner of the American Legion's annual oratorical contest. In 1960, at the age of thirty-five, he'd aroused the crowd as surprise keynoter at the Democratic National Convention.

December 1969 was when Cooper and Church tasted their first joint victory, in congressional approval of their initial amendment (to a Defense Appropriations act), prohibiting the use of funds for sending American ground combat troops into Laos or Thailand. Seeking application of such a ban to Cambodia became a raw challenge the following May, when the president without any congressional consultation ordered ground troops into that country.

Both senators exhibited their special talents in the months of maneuvering that followed. Once again, it was left to Church to announce the new plan of action, a Cooper-Church amendment to a military material-sales measure.

When Henry Kissinger said the nation should recognize that only the president could take us out of war and that this called for a national commitment—"almost an act of love"—Church observed tartly that what was needed was "not an act of love but an act of Congress." But meanwhile, with the astute assistance of Senators Mansfield and Aiken, Cooper was negotiating with the White House, probing better odds for passage of the amendment by softening its preamble so as to eliminate any suggestion of criticism of the executive. Cooper already had received over 8,000 pieces of mail, favorable in the main but painful where they were bitterly critical of his position. The administration remained adamant in its opposition, however, and both Cooper and Church took sharp blows in verbal encounter. Cooper's Republican Kentucky colleague, Senator Marlow Cook, (elected in 1968) said bitingly that, "Senators backing the Amendment are still salving their consciences for what they did in 1964. . . . They have found it was very easy to give authority for a wider Indochina war and now they find it is very hard to get out." But in January 1971 the second Cooper-Church amendment using the purse string power to limit the White House was passed by Congress.

Church's view of his partner in peacemaking was clear. In June of 1970, over Cooper's objections, he had introduced into the record an article in which, amid the senate storm over Cambodia, there was described "a quiet center where John Sherman Cooper is taking on all comers."

And when it came time in October of the following year for the Senate to lament Cooper's retirement, Church—unavoidably absent on tribute day—added a later statement. Its conclusion was as revealing of Church as of Cooper.

"The mark of Senator Cooper's real humanity is not to be found so much in legislative accomplishments (such as the Cooper-Church amendments) as in his persistent outspoken opposition to the American bombing in North Vietnam," Church said. "One of the first Senators to speak out in condemnation of the bombing, John

102

Sherman Cooper urged its cessation during the administration of Lyndon B. Johnson. His resolution did not falter after the renewal of the bombing by President Nixon.

"Indeed, as late as October 2 (of this year), he voted for an amendment that would have cut off funds for the bombing, not because he thought it would win the approval of Congress or even prove enforcible, but because he felt obliged to express his own feelings through his vote.

"He said: 'I vote for the amendment to express my feeling that I deplore this bombing and killing on both sides and I must say this as a human being. This is my only statement.' "

Cooper did not wait for the highwater mark of his peacemaking efforts in 1972 to confirm that he would not again run for the Senate. After all, it was a presidential election year. If someone were to renew the Republican hold on Cooper's senate seat, that newcomer would have to begin early. And as he has sometimes acknowledged, Cooper has tried to be a Kentucky politician around election seasons.

"Actually, I'd said on the night of my 1966 election that I wouldn't be a candidate again, but nobody believed me," he reminds. "Two years later people were saying to me skeptically, 'Did you say that!' "

Aside from his longtime hearing problem, a disability he refuses to give heed to, Cooper's health seemed good under normal duty pressures. He recognized and saluted the good work done into their eighties by the likes of George Aiken and Allen Ellender. But as he said later, "Whatever full mind one retained, I felt you also had to retain full energies. And there were new, complex problems demanding new solutions. It is almost a new world, not just a new era. I felt it needed one fresh, new mind. Besides, it would reduce my wife's burden and make me more than just a boarder for a change."

On January 21, 1972, at a Lexington meeting of the Kentucky Press Association, Cooper made the announcement that brought tears to hardened eyes, as to his and to his wife's. It was a short statement.

He was grateful to have been able to serve, he said.

"I believe you know I have worked hard for Kentucky and that I have endeavored to place national issues above party.

"I have faith in our country, its governmental system, and its people, and that our problems will be solved.

"I believe, as you do, that criticism directed to finding the truth is necessary, but that our country offers, and guarantees, greater individual freedom and opportunity than any in the world.

"Our system of government is a delicate one, depending in great measure on the respect of its three branches for each other and trust of the people in their government and in each other."

He concluded with words from Lincoln:

"Thanks to all! for the great republic—for the principle it lives by and keeps alive—for men's vast future—thanks to all!"

And then, before returning to Washington for more sixteen-hour workdays, he went to be cheered by a visit to Somerset where they know best what John Sherman Cooper means when he says there are two things which identify the Kentuckian: "one is that you always find red clay on our shoes and the second is that we all want to come back home."

8

COVINGTON & BURLING in downtown Washington exudes the hushed, carpeted atmosphere of influence and certainty found only rarely even at the highest level of offices involved in the hurly-burly of the Congress of the United States.

For John Sherman Cooper, taking over the law firm's prestigious "Dean Acheson chair" in January 1973 appeared to be an ideal way to serve out the remainder of his working career. He accepted those foreign clients whose interests he could represent without using high-echelon friendships or compromising his well-known foreign policy principles. Even in his new job, he continued to track through the labyrinth of bureaucracy the personal social security and veterans' claims of those many Kentuckians who could not quite get it into their heads that John Sherman Cooper no longer was their man in Washington.

It probably should have been expected that Cooper, even at seventy-three, would not long rest easy as an establishment lawyer on the periphery of national tasks needing pursuit. In April 1974 word leaked out that upon the final arrangement of diplomatic relations between the United States and communist East Germany President Nixon planned to nominate Cooper as the first postwar ambassador to the other side of the imprisoning Berlin Wall. The assignment would require tact second only to that demanded of America's new ambassador in Peking,

David Bruce, an old friend whom the Coopers had visited early that year.

When Kentucky's former Senator Thruston Morton heard the news of the East Berlin prospect, he telephoned Cooper. "Why in hell are you going, John?" Morton asked. "You can't speak German and you can't hear English!"

Morton says he knew, of course, why Cooper was being asked: "It was logical for the administration. They could have sent a young, bilingual career guy—who'd promptly be forgotten. To send John Cooper was to make a profound impact on the people of Hungary and Poland as well as on the people of East Germany. John's to be commended. I'd have told them to stuff it."

During the unexpected number of months it took for Washington to exact final, minimum commitments from East Berlin, Richard Nixon gave way to Gerald Ford; it was from President Ford that Cooper's nomination came. During that period, an alerted Cooper began reading Charlemagne, Bismarck, and other makers of German history while Lorraine Cooper began adding German to her linguistic arsenal.

"A divided Germany and Berlin have always presented a danger to peace," Cooper said in a 1974 interview in his law office. "The task now is to reduce that danger within the framework of reality. If the negotiations prove successful and I am nominated and confirmed, Secretary Kissinger will expect me to work on the issues we agreed to negotiate. We will have to pursue the matter of freer access between the two Germanys, to settle the humanitarian cases of divided U.S.-GDR families, to seek fair East German indemnification of Jewish victims of the Nazis and property claims of American citizens—private and corporate."

He added, "I wouldn't be considering this if it wasn't such a new challenge, tied to old problems that have in them the seeds of nuclear confrontation. People everywhere have the same desire—to stop this endless confrontation. I hope I can contribute something."

Small signs of the aptness of Thruston Morton's prediction about the wisdom of choosing Cooper soon surfaced. In fact, they came within weeks after the arrival of the Coopers and Mrs. Cooper's Shih Tzu dog Lhasa, in December 1974, to take up residence at an East Berlin hotel pending readiness of a temporary ambassadorial residence. A *New York Times* report said that wherever Cooper went in his effort to learn the country, East Germans were treating him as "a patrician figure due the highest respect." He was only the second representative of a noncommunist country to be invited for discussions by Erich Honecker, the first secretary of East Germany's communist party and thus the real head of state. "It was because I represent the United States," Cooper explained.

In a letter from East Berlin at the beginning of July 1975 he told how it was going.

"Living in a Communist (or as called by all their Governments a 'Socialist') state is, as I expected, totally different from living in an open and free country like the United States," he wrote. "But I accepted the appointment to be ambassador as a responsibility for our country. I find the work interesting, the officials very correct. And while our systems of government and openness of society are entirely different, I will do my best to assist in the development of a stable and peaceful relationship between the two countries.

"This relationship will depend, in my judgment, on the relationship between the United States and the Soviet Union."

In February 1976 Kentuckians noted with casual interest the unexpected return of Ambassador Cooper from East Berlin, ostensibly to visit Somerset and to be present in Louisville for a Lincoln Day dinner speech by Vice President Nelson Rockefeller. No other public explanations were given. The fact is that Cooper in his usual quiet way had returned to Washington at his own behest to awaken American officials to the signs of a reviving Soviet toughness.

During a grueling fortnight, unattended by any publicity, he conferred privately with President Ford, Secretary Kissinger, and many other key people in the State Department. He also managed to visit fifty-six members of the Senate and the House of Representatives. Later, he said mildly, "Yes, they learned something. So did I."

The following month Murray Marder, longtime diplomatic reporter for the *Washington Post,* produced a major analytical piece that was headed "U.S. getting sterner in Soviet policy." It noted President Ford's dropping use of the word "detente" as being one index of a stiffening in official policy toward the Soviet Union. Marder reported that this "hardening line" was spreading independently among liberals in Congress. They had begun to see that American failure to rise to challenges of Soviet aggrandizement might jeopardize the bargaining positions necessary for further American-Soviet arms and trade agreements.

It is safe to assume that many of these liberals were among those visited by Cooper. To impute too much importance to the Cooper influence on that occasion would be unwise—but clearly, in his seventy-fourth year, Cooper was still an element to be reckoned with.

In his July 1975 letter from East Berlin, he had added that Lorraine Cooper was busy arranging for "the first Fourth of July celebration of our Independence Day ever held in the German Democratic Republic." It was like an ambassador plenipotentiary from the United States of America named John Sherman Cooper, born in Somerset, Kentucky, to think of mentioning that with unabashed, unsophisticated pride.

The man from Somerset still reaches out to find in his American past the insights needed to pursue universal understanding and peace. In his approach to the East

Germans, he still exercises that gentlemanly geniality of the Kentucky border politician that had already won over disagreeing countrymen and contrary foreign statesmen.

In his own eyes he remains, as he once said, "a country fellow who'd merely tried to learn his lessons well." It may not be a formula for others to follow in the pursuit of global influence. In the instance of John Sherman Cooper, it shows that the integrity, the decency, the compassion, the sense of history, and the sense of community that served the deprived of a small Kentucky town also serve the world.

A Note on Sources

IMPORTANT SEGMENTS of this book were drawn from the willingness of many people to offer their firsthand information, anecdotes, and insights.

Former United States senator and congressman as well as former national chairman of the Republican party, Thruston Morton of Kentucky confessed that it never before had occurred to him to assess the foreign policy career of John Sherman Cooper in terms of Cooper's state and regional antecedents. A luncheon interview with Morton in Louisville produced anecdotal support for the thesis.

In Washington, Senator Stuart Symington found himself, fifty-five years after their days at Yale, still reiterating his inability to produce any grounds for criticism of Cooper. Vermont's Senator George Aiken, as a venerable on the eve of retirement, took time to ponder anew the Cooper phenomenon. In view of Cooper's consistent refusal to "take advantage of opponents" in the Senate, Aiken remained mystified as to how the Kentuckian ever had been a success in university athletics.

Former Cooper foreign policy aide William G. Miller and former staff secretary Audrey Hatry obligingly cut into their load of new senate duties in order to dwell in admiring detail on the reasons Senator Cooper drew veneration from his staff despite an administrative operation that was a disorganized nightmare. Miller now serves Senator Church as staff chief of the Senate Select Committee investigating the CIA.

Lawrence Forgy was twice interviewed, once when financial vice president for the University of Kentucky and again after beginning law practice in Louisville. Forgy took himself back to younger years when Senator Cooper astonished a callow aide by taking him along to capital receptions to mingle with the likes of Averell Harriman and other dignitaries.

Barry Bingham, Sr., chairman of the board of the *Louisville Courier-Journal* and the *Louisville Times*, offered a bit of personal history in the process of recalling some of his dealings with Cooper. Bingham noted that he had written the 1952 editorial in which the Louisville newspapers reluctantly withheld endorsement of Cooper.

Interviews with Senator Cooper began in mid-1973 when Cooper was at Covington & Burling. Ms. Carla Berts, the senator's secretary at C & B, was unusually devoted in keeping a perennially absentminded employer to the appointment grindstone. Ms. Trudie Musson, Cooper's secretary at the Embassy in East Berlin, also gave invaluable assistance in securing illustrations and other information.

A principal, three-hour visit with Lorraine Cooper took place one weekend in Louisville. It was conducted in a sitting room graciously made available by Mayor and Mrs. Harvey Sloane, with whom Mrs. Cooper was staying. During the interview, Mrs. Cooper took time for a telephone call to her husband, during which she revealingly dissipated his guilt at not having joined her in Louisville because of fatigue.

As candidly and generously cooperative as Senator and Mrs. Cooper were throughout, they were surpassed by the helpfulness of the Cooper kin on North Main Street in Somerset. In particular, there was the day before Easter 1975 when two brothers and all four sisters gathered, with Cornelia (Mrs. Dick) Cooper as hostess, to evoke the family years, clippings, and mementos. "You're all trying to make John out such a saint!" Fostine Cooper Hardin exclaimed at one point, recalling that when as a young girl she was seeing a beau not approved by her parents, it was John who snitched.

Few competent volumes on the nation's foreign policy of the past thirty years have failed at least to mention the creative role of John Sherman Cooper. I found helpful *The Imperial Presidency* (Boston, 1973) by Arthur M. Schlesinger, Jr., *Ambassador's Journal: A Personal Account of the Kennedy Years* (Boston, 1969) by John Kenneth Galbraith, and *Kissinger* (Boston, 1974) by Marvin and Bernard Kalb.

Professor Richard Lowitt of the University of Kentucky history department was just emerging from the second volume of his two-part biography of Senator George Norris when he made useful suggestions to me, on his way to what may be the definitive biography of John Sherman Cooper.

Should Professor Lowitt pursue his project, surely he will find the same invaluable help that came my way from the University of Kentucky Archives where the Cooper papers are being assembled and where Charles Atcher and William Cooper were especially attentive. Material of value came also from the library of the *Louisville Courier-Journal* and the *Louisville Times,* where the work of some fine reporters has shed light on Cooper's career.

Others not mentioned here know who they are.